P9-DBI-398

Making MINIATURE FLOWERS
with Polymer Clay

Making MINIATURE FLOWERS *with* Polymer Clay

Barbara Quast

NORTH LIGHT BOOKS
CINCINNATI, OHIO

731.42
QUA

About the Author

Barbara Osterhus Mitchell Quast was born in Brooklyn, New York, into a family of Scandinavian descent, and has a brother and a sister. She is married to Army Colonel (retired) John Quast, and has one married daughter, Christine McElroy, and a grandson, Andrew.

She earned a bachelor of science degree from S.U.N.Y. at Oswego and a master of science degree from Brooklyn College. Barbara has been a nursery and elementary school teacher, a product manager for a computer company and is an artist, a craft designer and the sole proprietor of Barbara Quast Creations.

Barbara enjoys creating decorative home decor, gift and jewelry items. She enjoys the pleasure of working toward the mastery of many different art and craft skills. She also finds joy in teaching others, while at the same time, learning from them.

She is an ambassador for Plaid Enterprises and a member of the National Polymer Clay Guild, the Society of Craft Designers and the Society of Decorative Painters.

Making Miniature Flowers With Polymer Clay. Copyright © 1998 by Barbara Quast. Manufactured in China. All rights reserved. No part of this book may be reproduced in any form or by any electronic or mechanical means including information storage and retrieval systems without permission in writing from the publisher, except by a reviewer, who may quote brief passages in a review. Published by North Light Books, an imprint of F&W Publications, Inc., 1507 Dana Avenue, Cincinnati, Ohio 45207. (800) 289-0963. First edition.

Other fine North Light Books are available from your local bookstore, art supply store or direct from the publisher.

02 01 00 99 98   5 4 3 2 1

Library of Congress Cataloging-in-Publication Data

Quast, Barbara.
    Making miniature flowers with polymer clay / Barbara Quast.
        p.   cm.
    Includes index.
    ISBN 0-89134-821-2 (pbk. : alk. paper)
    1. Polymer clay craft. 2. Flowers in art. I. Title.
TT297.Q37 1998
731.4′2—dc21   98-10111
                                                   CIP

Edited by Kathryn Kipp and Joyce Dolan
Production Edited by Michelle Kramer
Interior and cover designed by Candace Haught
Cover photography by Pamela Monfort Braun/Bronze Photography
Interior photography on pages 2, 8, 10, 28, 52, 64, 72, 82, 92, 102 and 112 by Greg Grosse Photography

Dedication

To my mother, Helen Palmquist Osterhus, who, by example,
has lovingly taught us to appreciate God's blessings through faith,
the importance of family, the goodness of people, the mystery
and beauty of nature, the joy of lifelong learning, the wisdom in books
and the personal pleasure in the happiness and laughter of others.
She is still teaching us.

Acknowledgments

I would like to acknowledge my cherished family for their love,
support and encouragement: my husband, John Quast; my daughter
and her husband, Christine and Mark McElroy and my grandson,
Andrew, (Drew); Christine, Andy and Danny Foland; Betty, John and
Laural Osterhus; Thelma MacKay; Rebecca Quast; Kathy MacKay; Beth,
Steve, Alison, Janine, Justin and Ryan Shea.
Thank you to my wonderful mentors and friends, especially
Jean Chancelor, Vickie Brown, Ann Polizzi, Joan Pompa and Jean Fregeau.
A special heartfelt thanks to creative and talented editor
Kathy Kipp, who has guided me with her expertise from the beginning of
this book and who made it fun to write; to content editor, Joyce Dolan, for
her knowledge and diligence in bringing it all together; to production editor,
Michelle Kramer, for skillfully piloting this book through production; to
designer, Candace Haught, for her special artistic talent; and to senior
editor, Greg Albert, who saw the value in a book about polymer clay flowers.

Table of Contents

Introduction

Modeling polymer clay flowers has been a great source of pleasure for me for years. You, too, can create beautiful miniature flowers and leaves from polymer clay by following the simple step-by-step instructions in this book. You will see how surprisingly easy it is to create a bit of the loveliness of nature with your own hands.

Polymer clay is produced in a myriad of gorgeous colors that can be combined and recombined to form a spectrum of visual wonder. A flower's lifelike beauty can be sculpted from this medium because the clay can be pressed almost as thin as a real petal.

Since polymer clay can be baked in a regular home oven or toaster oven, no special kilns are needed. The clay itself is an inexpensive medium, and adults and children can enjoy the pleasure of creating with it.

The flowers are suitable for small arrangements, pictures, decorative boxes, picture frames and other home decor items. Beautiful jewelry, hair ornaments and other adornments can be sculpted. The floral miniatures you can make become wonderful handcrafted gifts that will be treasured by all who receive them.

MATERIALS & TECHNIQUES TO MAKE

Polymer Clay Flowers

All you really need to make polymer clay flowers is an oven or toaster oven, a baking pan, toothpicks and clay. In this chapter, I'll show you more supplies you can use and some of the basic techniques for working with clay.

Before you start the projects, read through the entire step-by-step instruction and assemble all the supplies needed for each project.

HOW TO USE THE INSTRUCTIONS IN THIS BOOK

1. Please read all of the instructions for a project before starting it.
2. The instructions are similar to recipes for cooking. Following the exact sequence of steps in the instructions can be crucial to the ease of using the clay and the quality of your final project.
3. A circle template is a useful tool in determining the sizes of the unflattened and flattened balls of clay. The diagrams of the diameters of circles, page 17 in the instructions, can be photocopied and used as a guideline.

Materials

Supplies for making polymer clay flowers and leaves are available from retail stores, such as M.J. Designs, Michael's, Pearl, A.C. Moore, Ben Franklin, Total Crafts, Frank's Nursery and Crafts and Wal-Mart. See Sources for Materials in the back of this book for further information.

Polymer Clay—Promat, FIMO, Sculpey III, Friendly Clay and Cernit are excellent choices for making flowers. I use all the brands available to me because each has a lovely palette of colors. If extra strength is required, I mix white Promat with the other brands when I am tinting the colors from dark to light.

Handi-Tak—Handi-Tak is available at the previously mentioned stores and is wonderful for temporarily adhering flowers and leaves to an object. Handi-Tak is also useful when designing an arrangement because it will hold the components in place until they are glued to a surface, it does not leave spots after it has been removed and it can be used over and over again.

Goop—Goop glue is great for attaching flowers to jewelry findings and other surfaces. It creates an excellent bond. There is a label on the package warning the consumer not to heat it.

Tacky Glue—I use Plaid Tacky Glue, a white glue that is useful for gluing flowers to surfaces. It is wonderful for gluing together baked and unbaked flower components. Since there is not a warning label about heating, I use it in the creation of many flowers before baking. I also use it in bakers' clay.

Acrylic Paints—Acrylic paints are used for painting details on the flowers and for color washes on petals and leaves. FolkArt is my favorite brand because of its pigmentation and open time. I use it for coloring bakers' clay, too.

Dry-Brush Stencil Paint—Dry-Brush Stencil Paint by Plaid, when used sparingly on a stencil brush or eye shadow applicator, creates beautiful, subtle shading on baked petals and leaves. I find it easier to control the amount of color with Dry-Brush Stencil Paint than with acrylic paints.

Crepe Paper—White crepe paper is used to impress natural looking texture onto flower petals. White is used because there is no danger of the color bleeding. I prefer the folded type of crepe paper over the rolls because the texture on the folded type is less pronounced.

Cookie Sheet or Other Baking Surface—Use a cookie sheet or another baking surface to hold the clay during baking. If the surface of the cookie sheet is too slick, a component of the clay may form an undesirable shiny bottom on your leaf or flower. This can be avoided by baking your creations on paper plates, index cards, or leftover pieces of framer's mat board placed on the shiny surface of the cookie sheet. Stoneware plates can also be used.

Kemper Tools—Kemper tools are used for cutting out the flower shapes. The packages are marked with the tools' cutting dimensions. Friendly Cutters, from American Art Clay, Wilton Gum Paste

Cutters, and aspic and canape cutters, from cake and candy supply shops, can also be used.

Paper Punch—Use a paper punch to cut holes in the index card and waxed paper work surfaces.

Floral Stem Wire and Tape—Flower stem wire and floral tape are readily available in the flower arranging department of the previously mentioned stores. I usually use cloth-covered stem wire because it bonds better with the clay than the uncovered stem wire. I gear the gauge of wire to the size of my flower. For example, I use a very thin wire, gauge no. 24 to no. 26, for tiny flowers and thicker wire, gauge no. 18, for roses. The wrapping of floral tape around the stem wire will increase the girth of the stem and is used to attach flowers, buds, leaves and branches. It is produced in dark green, leaf green, lime green, brown and white.

Emery Board—An emery board is used to smooth any rough baked edges. Sometimes, I lightly use the abrasion of the emery board to remove any lint or dark specks that have become embedded in the surface of the clay.

Wooden Tool—A wooden tool is useful for hollowing out the trumpet of a daffodil. It is found in the clay and ceramic tool department of craft stores.

Brayer—A brayer or rolling pin can be used interchangeably. I usually sit in a comfortable chair and work on a tray in my lap. The brayer is easier to use in a confined space.

Sieve—A sieve is used to make criss-cross markings for certain flower centers. It can be plastic or metal. Sieves are produced in different sizes of mesh, so I have several. For example, a tea strainer is great for the centers of very tiny flowers. Window screen or tulle can also be used for centers.

Additional Supplies—The following items are also useful: craft knife, cuticle scissors, scissors, toothpicks, magnifying glass, hair combs, waxed paper, index cards, aluminum foil and sandwich bags.

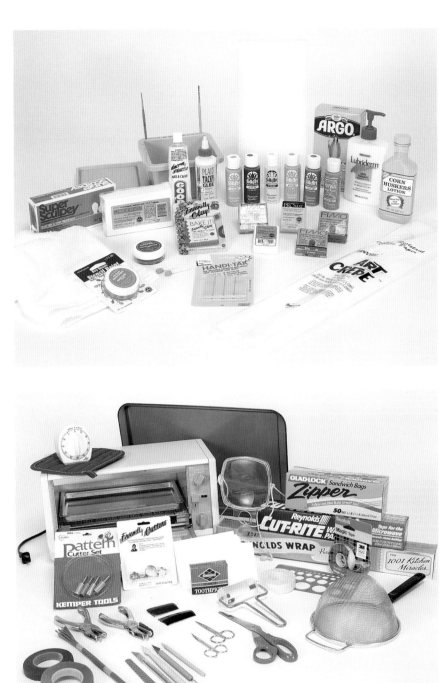

The supplies needed for making miniature polymer clay flowers are readily available. Almost everyone has a kitchen oven or toaster oven, and many of the tools and supplies needed are household items. Polymer clays, paints and floral materials are available at arts and crafts supply stores.

Polymer Clay

I use all of the brands of polymer clay available to me for making flowers. They are Promat, FIMO, Sculpey III, Friendly Clay and Cernit. Each brand has unique colors and varying characteristics.

Mix brands to increase the color selection and to vary the strength and texture of the clay. For example, when making pastel-colored flowers I often use Promat White with other brands to lighten them and make tints. Promat alone or used with other brands makes a strong, thin flower. By mixing brands, your color choices are unlimited and you can enjoy using the many lovely colors available in every brand.

FIMO is almost as strong as Promat, and most of my leaves are made from FIMO Leaf Green with slight color variations made by adding colors from other brands.

For making tools, and for leaf veining and texture molds, I use Super Sculpey.

Clean Your Hands

It's important to wash your hands before working with polymer clay because the clay picks up lint and other invisible debris that might be noticeable after the flower is formed or baked.

Cleansing your hands when changing from one color family to another is a must because color from the clay you were using adheres to your hands. For example, if you're making green leaves and you switch to making white flower petals without cleaning your hands, you might end up with mint green petals instead of white.

If you prefer, instead of washing your hands between color families, you can rub your hands with hand lotion and then wipe them dry with a paper towel or an old terry cloth towel.

Knead and Store Polymer Clay

I knead polymer clay with both my hand and the clay inside a plastic food storage bag. The heat from my hand heats up the inside of the bag, which speeds up the softening of the clay. If you have trouble softening polymer clay, use some FIMO Mix Quick or Friendly Clay Super Softener. Another good reason to use the storage bag is that if the clay is crumbly, the pieces stay contained in the bag.

I store my clay in the plastic bag I mixed it in, labeling the bag with the mixtures, brands and color names.

I have many mixtures, so I keep all the mixed clays for each color family in a larger, separate, clear, gallon-size, plastic food storage bag. For example, I keep all my yellows together by placing the separate, smaller bags of yellow clay inside the larger, gallon-size, clear plastic bag.

Bake the Clay

Bake the flowers and leaves that don't have stems on an index card or a mat board scrap placed on a cookie sheet, a stoneware plate, or directly on a cookie sheet that has a dull finish. Sometimes the clay forms a shiny, clear, uneven glazing on the bottom if the surface of the baking sheet is slick.

Stemmed Flowers—When baking flowers on tall stems, I bend the stems in half or fourths and poke them into crumpled aluminum foil to bake. Be careful when using a toaster oven for the taller stemmed flowers because it's easy to overbake them. The inside of the toaster oven is small, so the flowers baked on stems may be too close to the upper element and scorch, causing irritating fumes, as well as ruining your work. You can also bend the blossoms over so they are closer to the lower part of the oven.

Baking Time—The thickness and brand of the clay will be the major factors in deciding how long to bake your project and at what temperature. The projects in this book give an estimated time for baking at the temperature suggested by the manufacturer of the clay. Always check the directions on the package for the proper time and temperature for a particular brand of clay.

Oven temperatures vary, so it's often a matter of experimentation. An oven gauge is handy, and inexpensive, for checking the actual temperature of your oven.

Your flowers and leaves are still soft when hot from the oven. They'll harden when cool.

Caution: Do not overbake the clay, as irritating fumes can be emitted. Read the directions on the package.

TIP

Your clay can bake or cure to hardening in a hot car in the summer, so keep that in mind while traveling. ❧

Get to Know Your Clay

A little manipulation of the clay before starting an actual project is a beneficial warm-up, especially for beginners. Once you are in the throes of making a flower, it's good to be knowledgeable about what your clay can and cannot do. Practice will also make it easier to follow the individual instructions.

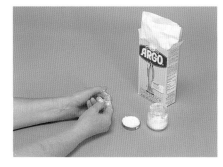

Hand lotion and a terry cloth towel keep your hands clean. Your hands stay soft too! Rub cornstarch on your fingers to keep polymer clay from sticking to them.

1. First, start without cornstarch, and make the thinnest petals you can manipulate with your fingers. Then, rub cornstarch on your hands and fingertips and make very thin petals. The cornstarch makes it easier to handle the clay by keeping it from sticking to your fingers. It also tends to stiffen the clay.

2. Rub a little cornstarch in a circle on an index card.

3. Press a piece of clay onto the circle on the index card. Using a single-edged razorblade, holding the blade

almost horizontal, scrape or peel off the petal. It's even easier when you put your razorblade into the cornstarch before removing your petal from the index card.

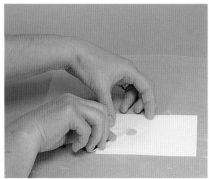

4. With a piece of clay flattened on an index card, press textured markings into the petal with a toothpick. Remove the clay from the card with a razorblade. Press the petal again to make softer indentations and to improve the edges.

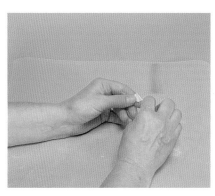

5. Press textured markings onto the flattened petal while holding the clay on your index finger.

Form the Basic Flower Shapes

Ball: To make a ball, roll a piece of clay between your palms. If the ball is very tiny, it may be easier to roll between the pads of your fingers.

Teardrop: A teardrop is made from a ball. Roll one end of the ball until that end is narrow and thin. Sometimes you'll want it to be narrow and rounded; other times a more prominent point is required for the tip of a teardrop.

Coil: Roll a small piece of clay between your palms until it's long and thin. You can also roll the clay on the table with the palm of one hand. For an exceptionally even coil, roll the clay with a flat surface, such as an index card or a piece of cardboard.

IF CLAY STICKS TO YOUR FINGERS

- Rub your fingers with a bit of cornstarch.
- Rub your hands with a dry paper towel or an old terry cloth towel to remove some of the clay. The clay sometimes lodges in the whorls of your fingerprints, and the clay you're working with sticks to the clay on your fingers.
- Rub some hand lotion onto your fingers and rub it and the clay off with paper towels or a terry cloth towel.
- The clay may be too soft. Let it sit for a few minutes to cool, put it into the refrigerator, or mix in some cooler clay.

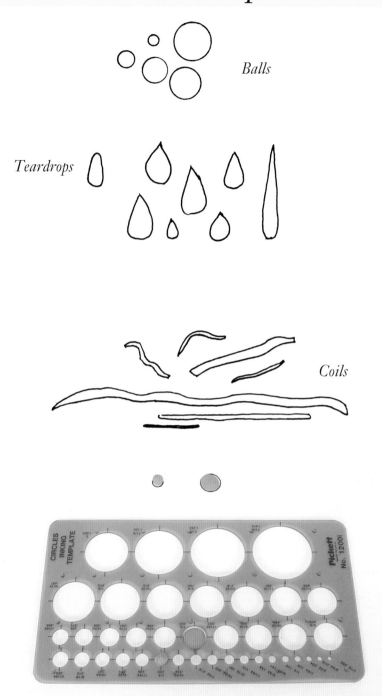

Balls

Teardrops

Coils

Diameter Circles Template

A circle template makes it easy to determine the amount of clay to use. You can make a copy of the opposite page, which shows a template of circles of varying diameters.

Diameters of Circles

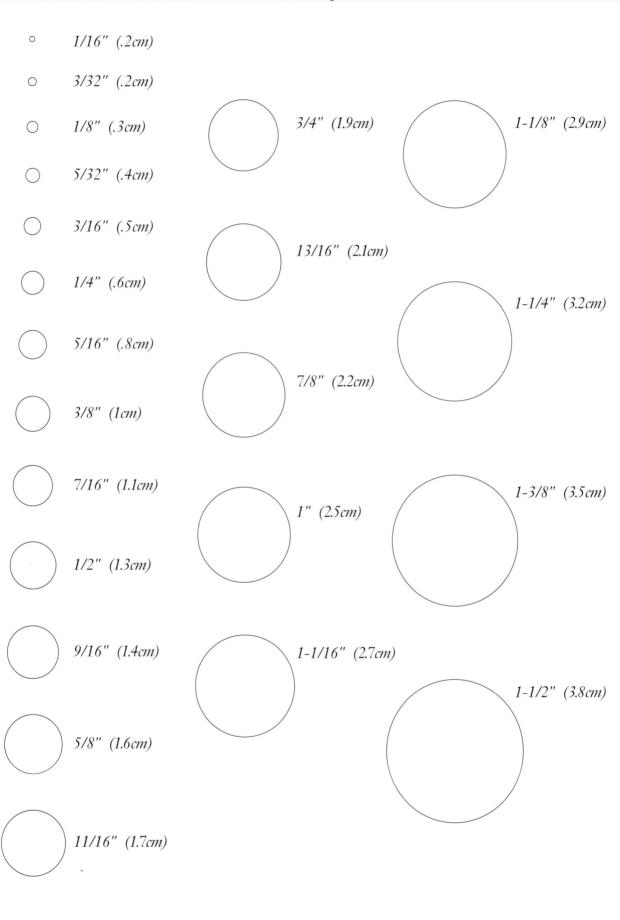

1/16" (.2cm)

3/32" (.2cm)

1/8" (.3cm)

5/32" (.4cm)

3/16" (.5cm)

1/4" (.6cm)

5/16" (.8cm)

3/8" (1cm)

7/16" (1.1cm)

1/2" (1.3cm)

9/16" (1.4cm)

5/8" (1.6cm)

11/16" (1.7cm)

3/4" (1.9cm)

13/16" (2.1cm)

7/8" (2.2cm)

1" (2.5cm)

1-1/16" (2.7cm)

1-1/8" (2.9cm)

1-1/4" (3.2cm)

1-3/8" (3.5cm)

1-1/2" (3.8cm)

Divide Circles Into Sections to Make Petals

I often suggest using cutters or patterns for flower shapes, but it is possible to make any number of petaled flowers by dividing a flat circle into sections, leaving the middle uncut. The sections are then cut into petals.

Although we should try to cut the sections evenly, it is only necessary to cut them approximately the same size. The clay will stretch and be pinched, and the size of each petal can be adjusted when further along in the process of making the flower.

To Make Three Petals:

1. Make an indentation in the circle's center with a toothpick.
2. Make one cut toward the center.
3. Make another cut toward the center at about one-third of the way around the circle (less than halfway around the circle).
4. Cut the large portion in half. You will end up with three sections.

To Make Four Petals:

1. Make an indentation in the circle's center with a toothpick.

2. Divide the circle in half.
3. Divide each half in half again, into four sections.

To Make Five Petals:

1. Make an indentation in the circle's center with a toothpick.
2. Make one cut toward the center.
3. Make a second cut into the center at a point less than half of the diameter of the circle away from the first cut, keeping in mind that you want five approximately equal sections.
4. Divide the larger part into three sections.
5. Divide the smaller part in half. You will end up with five sections.

To Make Six Petals:

1. Make an indentation in the circle's center with a toothpick.
2. Divide the circle in half.
3. Cut each half into three sections, as equal as possible.

To Make Eight Petals:

1. Make an indentation in the circle's center with a toothpick.

2. Divide the circle into halves, and then into fourths.
3. Divide each fourth in half, into eight sections.

To Make Sixteen Petals:

1. Make an indentation in the circle's center with a toothpick.
2. Divide the circle into halves, fourths, and then into eighths.
3. Divide each eighth in half, into sixteen sections.

CUT PETALS INTO SECTIONS

When cutting the petals, be sure to find the center of the outer edge of the petal and cut on either side of that, into the previous cuts. By finding the center of each section edge, you will be able to cut more even petals.

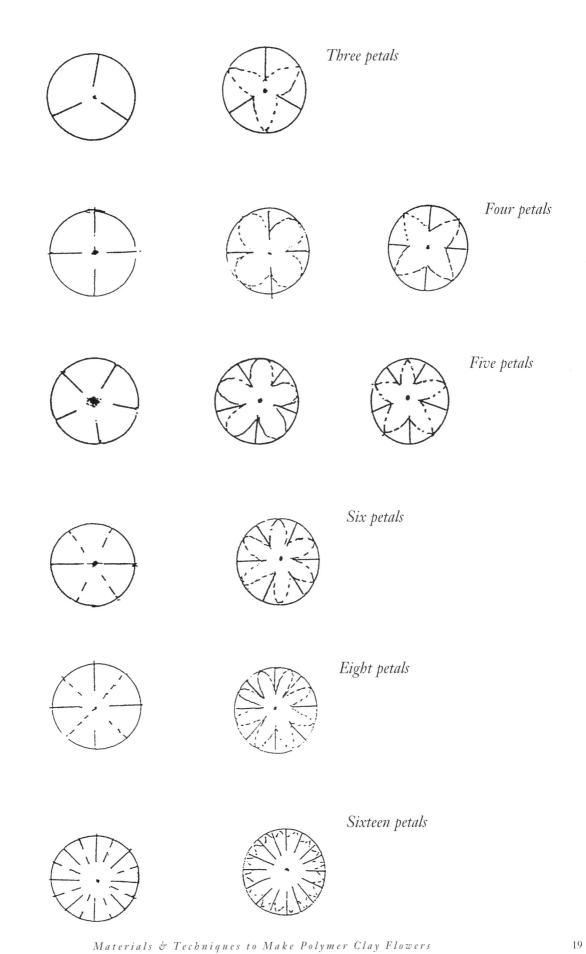

Three petals

Four petals

Five petals

Six petals

Eight petals

Sixteen petals

Prebake Flower Parts

Prebaking some of the flower parts is advantageous because it allows you to combine parts that might lose their impressed designs if you press them in place while they're soft. For example, if you want to add a yellow center to a daisy, it's easier to press in, or to glue on, a hard, prebaked center without losing the impression or flattening it.

You can make several centers at a time when you prebake and then store them without worry of damage. It's also faster to make several at one time.

The hardened prebaked clay can be easier to work with when joining soft unbaked flower parts. You don't have to be as careful about distortion. Prebaked clay provides a more stable base for attaching unbaked clay. It can also be used as an armature.

When prebaked centers are pressed into a tiny flower center, the hardened clay often combines with the soft unbaked clay. But if this doesn't happen and you can't apply enough pressure without distorting the flower, it's better to place a dab of white glue or tacky white glue between the surfaces to be joined. Read the instructions on the glue label to be sure there's not a warning about heating the glue. Most white glues don't have a warning.

Prebake flower centers to make attaching them a cinch. Use white glue to adhere baked and unbaked clay together securely.

The thinnest petals look the most lifelike, but they are also the most fragile. If a flower is framed behind glass or in domes, you need not be as concerned, but if a project will be handled frequently, such as jewelry or a coffee table arrangement, stronger petals are important. There are a number of ways you can strengthen a petal while maintaining a fragile look.

Center Thick, Edges Thin

The center core of the petal should be slightly thicker than the outside edges. All petals should have their edges thinned. Thinning the edges will hide the actual thickness and make a sturdier flower look more fragile.

Be careful that when you thin a petal, you don't accidentally thin the center too much. If you hold your petal up to the light, you'll be able to see if the center is thinner than the edge of your petal because more light will shine through where it's thinnest.

Cushioning

The arrangement, shape and length of the petals are factors in choosing the best method to strengthen the flower. Thin, narrow daisy petals are delicate because they have little support, whereas the structure of the rose gives a solid base for the wider, rounded, thin rose petals and edges.

You can create a protective pillow for petals like the daisy by pressing already baked or unbaked flowers down onto a softened green clay background or onto unbaked leaves. When baked, they will be one strong piece with cushioning for the delicate flower parts.

The pansy adapts well to cushion-ing. Make the pansy flat, with the back and side petals large and rounded so they make a strong unit with the bottom petals acting as cushion for the top petals.

Other Strengthening Methods

Mix some transparent clay in with the clay so that light will shine through, or allow the background to be seen through the petals to give a further illusion of thinness.

Placing a white stem wire in the center of a petal to act as a rib or vein can also make a petal stronger.

A petal base on a stem, even if it doesn't reach far into the petal, also makes the flower stronger. If the flower petal gets knocked, the stem wire will move and the petal won't snap.

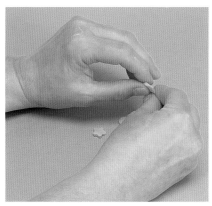

These shapes have unthinned edges. The thickness of the clay is clearly visible.

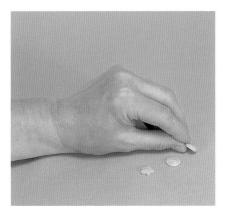

Press and thin the edges to hide the thickness of the flower or petal.

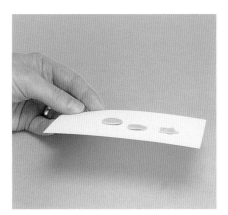

The blunt edges on these shapes have been thinned to create the illusion of thinness.

Thin, baked blossoms can be cushioned by soft clay and rebaked. The blossoms will be stronger.

Color

You can make flowers look beautiful and natural by using several tints or shades of color in one flower or arrangement. For example, if you start with one brand and color of red clay and add white clay, you can achieve graduated shades of pink without worry of clashing.

When experimenting, mix only a small amount of clay. Take note of the proportions, e.g., 2 parts white to 1 part red. Mixing small amounts takes less time and you'll not end up with large amounts of clay in a color you can't use.

Keep a Record of Color Mixtures

Here is a method I've found helpful to keep track of color mixtures.
1. When you open a new color of clay, record the brand name and the color on the top of a loose-leaf notebook page.
2. Then, make a small, three-petaled rosebud with the original color. Slice off the bottom of the rose with a single-edged razorblade to make a flat base.
3. Then, add white to the red and make a rosebud of that color. Keep adding more white, record the proportions and make a rosebud in each tint, until you have a row of rosebuds in graduating values from dark to light.
4. Bake the rosebuds and then glue them in the graduated sequence onto the piece of loose-leaf paper in step 1. You could also use white glue to fasten the unbaked rosebuds onto a labeled index card and, after they're baked and cool, tape the card onto the loose-leaf paper.

It might seem like a lot of work to make rosebuds when it seems that just a flattened piece of clay would do, but the shadows created by the petals make matching one color to another easier. For example, each brand has its own white clay. Some brands lean more to the creamy yellow side and some to the gray side.

I often mix two colors or brands together to form a different color. By adding graduated amounts of white to that, I have created a completely different range of colors. Keeping a record of all these combinations is a great reference for matching colors or finding particularly pleasing combinations. I don't have to say to myself, "How did I get that wonderful peach color?"

Simple Principles of Color Mixing

An artist's cardboard color wheel is very useful when mixing colors. Most color wheels provide instructions.

Use a color wheel when you want to drab, or make less intense, a bright color. Colors opposite each other on the color wheel drab each other. For example, if you don't have leaf green clay take a brighter green and add a little red, its opposite on the color wheel, and the green will magically become less vibrant and more realistic for a leaf.

Remember, the same rule applies when painting details or shading on petals and leaves. For example, the combination of yellow and purple when painting a pansy face will drab both colors down, so you might need several coats of paint to get the color face you want. You can block in the area of the face you want to paint with a little white paint first, to act as a barrier between the colors.

Color Reference Guide

Take time to make a reference guide of the different brands and colors of clay. This can save time in the long run. By adding increasing amounts of white, and/or other colors, you can create a tremendous range of colors. By keeping a record of your mixtures, you won't need to guess when creating a duplicate or a variation of a color you wish to use for a project.

Add a small amount of red to bright green to create a duller more leafy green.

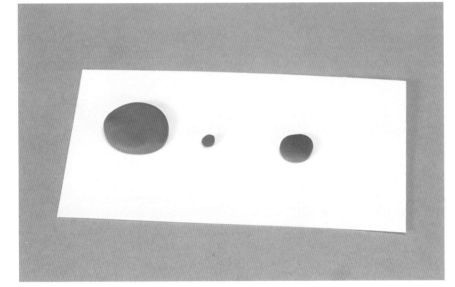

Drab Colors

Strange as it may seem, by mixing a small amount of the color opposite a color on the color wheel, you can tone down the color almost magically. For example:
1. To tone down green, add a small amount of red; to tone down red, add a small amount of green.
2. To tone down yellow, add a small amount of violet; to tone down violet, add a small amount of yellow.
3. To tone down orange, add a small amount of blue; to tone down blue add a small amount of orange.

Other Tips and Techniques

Height Adjusters

For a more natural look and interesting design, you'll want certain types of flowers that aren't on stems at different levels or heights. The dogwood is a good example of a circumstance where height adjusters make for a more interesting design.

To make height adjusters:
1. Roll a coil of clay about ¼" (0.6cm) in diameter.
2. Slice off pieces in different widths.
3. Bake.
4. Glue height adjusters under flowers on flat surfaces, so that some petals can be placed over and others under other flower's petals.

Leaf Veining Molds

Doesn't making your own leaf veining molds sound like a daunting process? In actuality, it is about as simple as pressing the back of a real leaf onto a flat piece of clay. You then bake that piece of clay until it is hard. Take a paintbrush or your finger and rub a little cornstarch onto the hardened mold. Take another piece of flattened clay and press it onto the leaf mold. This is called a reverse mold. Bake your reverse mold of the leaf veins. This is the mold you will use when you want to impress leaf veins. Keep the original mold too, because you can use it if you want to make more reverse molds. I usually use Super Sculpey for making molds.

You can also make molds by impressing the clay with a pin to make veins that look like the veins of a real leaf. Make the leaf mold of veins quite a bit longer than the actual clay leaf you wish to vein. You can use different parts of the mold for different leaves so they all do not look exactly the same. Bake the mold. You then have to put a little cornstarch on the original mold and press another piece of flattened clay onto that, forming a reverse mold. Bake your reverse mold and you are all set.

The veins in many leaves are similar. I consider the veining for the rose leaf generic veining, which can be used for many leaves. You can use leaf molds from many different kinds of leaves. For example, celery leaves have veining similar to pansy leaves.

Clean the Clay Flowers

For most of the flowers, cleaning is easy. Gently swish the flowers back and forth in cool to lukewarm soapy water. Rinse by gently swishing the flower back and forth in clear water. Let the flowers air dry.

If your flower center is made from threads and you wish to be able to wash these, treat the threads with sealer before making the flower.

EDIBLE FLOWERS

The techniques in this book for making polymer clay flowers can be adapted for cake decorating. You can use gum paste mix or marzipan for sugar-based flowers. You can find what you need at craft, candy-making and cake-decorating supply shops. Marzipan is usually available at grocery stores.

How to Wrap a Floral Stem

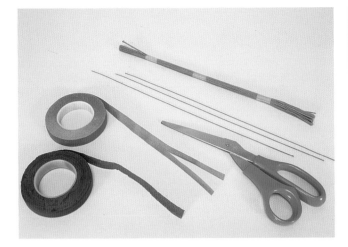

1. Materials: floral stems, scissors, green and brown floral tape.

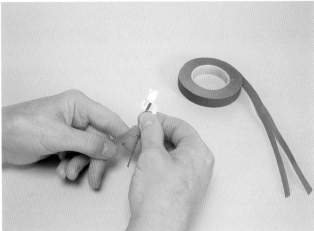

2. Split the floral tape in half. Begin wrapping near the flower.

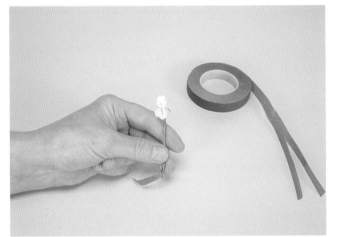

3. Continue wrapping to the end of the stem.

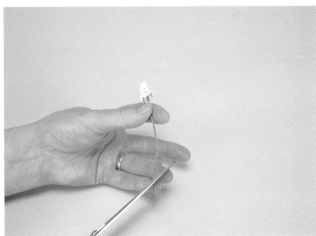

4. Snip and clean ends.

Bakers' Clay

I now work mostly with polymer clay because it's more durable, doesn't need sealing and comes in ready-made, beautiful colors. But before I started using it, I made flowers with bakers' clay.

Bakers' clay is a great medium for flowers. You can obtain beautiful results with it. You don't bake it; it cures in the air in about two days. Baking can make the petals crack. It's surprisingly strong and can be pressed very thin. It's inexpensive to make, fun to work with and can be refrigerated in a moldable state plastic bag for many weeks. The fact that it does not have to be baked can be an advantage, in some instances. I highly recommend you try it.

Hand Lotion and Cornstarch

Hand lotion and cornstarch are useful in the same way with bakers' clay as they were with polymer clay. For most of the flowers, you can follow the same directions.

Prepare Bakers' Clay

1. Carefully tear the crusts off the bread. Look over the bread and remove any brown crumbs.
2. Open the plastic bag and roll the top down so it makes a bowl.
3. Put the bread into the open plastic bag and then, tear the bread into little pieces.
4. Add 3 tbsp. of tacky white glue and 1 tsp. of glycerine. Working with your hand inside the plastic bag, mix and squeeze the bread, glue and glycerine together. Keep kneading and squeezing. You'll probably need to add a little cornstarch and rub cornstarch on your hands. It'll be messy! At some time you may have to wash your hands and then continue the mixing.
5. After squeezing and mixing, the mixture becomes a smooth clay that doesn't stick to your hands.
6. Discard the plastic bag.
7. Add the white acrylic paint to the clay and mix it until it's dispersed. The clay without white paint added dries to the color of macaroni. This macaroni color interferes with the purity of the colors that you mix into the bakers' clay.
8. Place the clay into a small sandwich bag, seal it and store it in the refrigerator.

WHAT YOU'LL NEED

- 3 slices of white bread (It does not have to be fresh)
- 1 tsp. glycerine
- 1 tsp. white acrylic paint
- 3 tbsp. tacky white glue
- Quart (liter) or gallon (4 liter), sturdy, plastic food storage bag
- Cornstarch
- Hand lotion
- Old terry towel, dampened
- Toothpicks

Color

Add acrylic paint, dry-brush stencil paint or oil paints to make different shades and colors. Store each color in a separate sealed bag. Keep them together in a larger sealed bag in the refrigerator.

Stems

It's best to use cloth-covered stem wire that will not rust. Candy-making suppliers carry these stems. If you can't find the kind that won't rust, dip the tip and upper portion of the stem, which will be covered with bakers' clay, into clear nail polish to create a barrier between the stem and the clay.

Glue

When adding petals to a flower, or a stem to a leaf, you need to use tacky glue to make the clay adhere together. For example, if you're making a rose, you have to put glue around the base of each petal added.

Premake Parts of the Flower

You'll need to premake and allow to dry the same parts of a flower that you would prebake if you were working with polymer clay. This hardens the bakers' clay so that it's easier to work with.

Seal

It's not absolutely necessary to seal bakers' clay, but to be on the safe side, I usually do.

Spray Bakers' Clay Flowers With Sealer

1. I prefer Testors Dull Cote which gives the flowers a bisque look. I use two or three coats on the flowers and leaves.
2. On toothpicks, poke your flowers close together, but not touching, onto a Styrofoam block. By doing this, you can spray twenty or more roses at one time. By turning the Styrofoam block, and raising and lowering it, you can cover all the flowers' sides, bases and crevices.
3. Start spraying away from your flowers, and then move the spray onto them. For flowers in frames, I usually use two coats. For jewelry, I usually spray the flowers three times.
4. Place loose flowers and leaves, wrong side up, on a doubled over piece of masking tape to hold them in place and then spray. When they're dry, turn them over and spray the top side.

Arrange and Mount

Believe it or not, all the flowers and leaves shown below were made with bakers' clay. I simply arranged and glued them to an ivory moiré background, then placed a double oval matboard over it.

Roses

We can all appreciate the beauty of a rose. This beloved flower, affectionately called the queen of flowers, is a joy to create with polymer clay and is much easier to make than one can imagine.

There are many varieties of roses. We will begin by making a basic rose. Later in this chapter, other ways of making roses will be shown. They are a little more complex, but still easy to do. Making a basic rose is simply a matter of pressing small balls of clay flat into petals and pressing the bases of these petals around a clay center that's been hardened by prebaking. The basic pink rose is constructed by pressing three layers of petals around the prebaked center, while using the attached toothpick or floral stem wire as a holder. The pre-baked center and the first layer of petals are made from dark pink, the next layer from a medium shade of pink and the outside layer with a light pink. You begin with the center and work your way out to the outermost layer of petals.

The more gradually the petal colors shade from dark to light, the more subtle the finished rose. You will want color change, but often you will not want a strong contrast between the inner and outer petals.

Of course, you can use just one shade for the whole rose, but the transition from dark to light makes the rose more interesting and natural looking.

WHAT YOU'LL NEED

- White clay
- Red clay
- Leaf green clay
- Aluminum foil
- Cookie sheet
- Oven or toaster oven
- Block of Styrofoam
- Toothpicks
- Tacky white glue

- Scissors
- Waxed paper
- Fine-toothed comb
- Real or plastic leaf, a mold of a leaf, or a straight pin for veining the leaf
- Floral tape (optional)
- Cloth-covered stem wire (optional)
- Brown, burgundy or dark green acrylic paint or dry-brush stencil paint

for shading leaves or painting buds (optional)
- Green acrylic paint, similar in color to the stem wire, for painting buds (optional)
- Acrylic paint or dry-brush stencil paint, a darker shade of the bud color, for painting buds (optional)

Make Basic Rose Centers

1 Prepare the Clay

1. Knead three balls of white clay (about ¾" to 1" [1.9cm to 2.5 cm] in diameter each).
2. Add a marble-size ball of red clay to one white ball to make a ball of clay that is a slightly dark pink. If the pink is too dark, add more white. If it's too light, add more red.
3. Add a smaller amount of red to the second ball to make a medium shade of pink.
4. Add less red to the third ball to make it light pink. We now have three shades of pink clay.

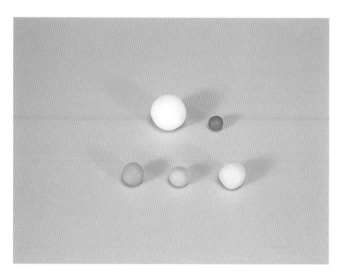

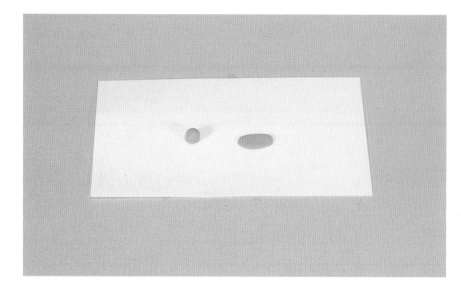

2 Start With Dark Pink Clay

1. Make a ³⁄₁₆" to ¼" (0.5cm to 0.6cm) ball of dark pink clay.
2. Flatten this into an elongated round shape between the pads of your thumb and forefinger. Be particularly careful to thin the edges. The shape does not have to be exactly symmetrical.

3 Roll the Center

Starting at one end, roll the flattened shape between your thumb and forefinger, jelly roll fashion, from one end to the other.

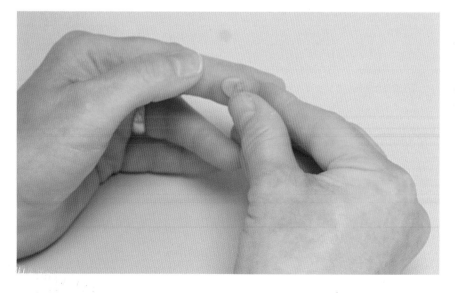

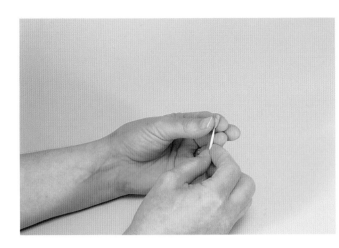

4 Insert a Toothpick

1. Carefully push the base of your center onto a toothpick. If you want to make a rose on a stem, dip the tip of a piece of covered stem wire into white glue and carefully push the base of the rose center onto the glued tip of the stem wire.
2. For convenience, make several rose centers at one time.

5 Prepare to Bake the Centers

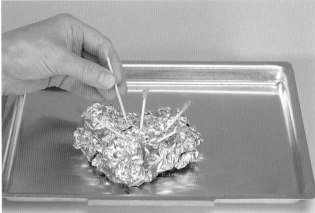

1. Preheat the oven to the temperature suggested by the manufacturer of your clay.
2. Crumple up a sheet of aluminum foil and place it on a pan or cookie sheet.
3. Stick the toothpicks with the rose centers into the crumpled aluminum foil to hold them in place.

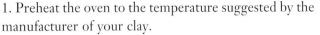

TIP

If you are using a toaster oven, be careful to place your rose in the aluminum foil at an angle away from the top of the oven, so that it does not get close to the upper element of the oven and scorch. 🍂

6 Bake the Centers

Bake the centers for twenty minutes. Let them cool for three to five minutes. It's easier to form a rose around a hardened center.

First Layer of Petals

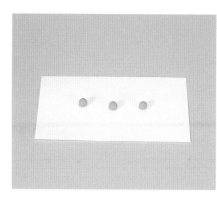

TIP

When you do not need to have the rose in your hand, place the toothpick or stem wire into a block of Styrofoam.

7 Form Balls of Clay

Form three ³⁄₁₆″ (0.5cm) balls of dark pink clay for the three petals in the first, or innermost, layer.

8 Dab White Glue Onto the Base of the Center

Use a toothpick to dab a tiny amount of tacky white glue onto the lower part of the prebaked center. This is the only time you will need glue because the other unbaked clay petals will adhere to each other.

9 Flatten the First Petal

Flatten one ball into a round shape, using the pads of your thumb and forefinger, making sure to thin the edges.

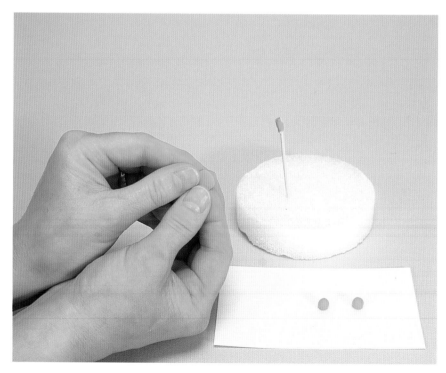

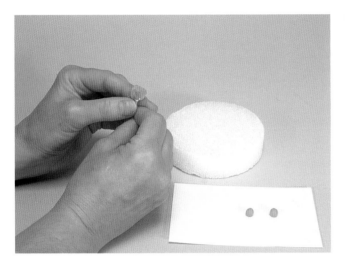

10 Attach the First Petal

With your forefinger, press the lower portion of the first petal over the glue on the prebaked center.

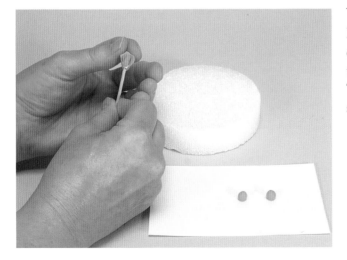

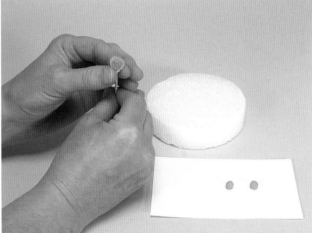

11 Secure the First Petal

With your thumb and forefinger, curve the lower portion of the petal around the base of the prebaked center.

12 Flare the Petal Edge

Flare the top edge of the petal slightly, using a pinching, downward movement with the tips and pads of your thumb and forefinger. Do not pinch the edges together. The flared top edges should be about even with, or slightly higher than, the top of the prebaked center.

TIP

If you get glue on your fingers, wipe them off on a damp towel. 🌹

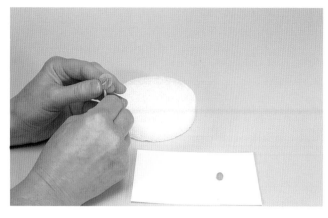

13 Attach the Second Petal

Flatten the second ball of dark pink clay into a petal and press the lower edge around the prebaked center. Leave room for one more petal to overlap these two petals.

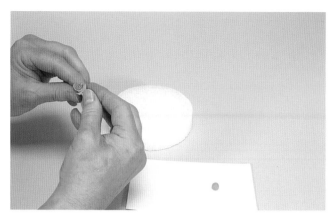

14 Flare the Petal Edge

Slightly flare the edge of the second petal, as you did the first one.

15 Attach the Third Petal

Flatten the third ball of dark pink clay into a petal. Press the lower edges of the petal over the prebaked center, overlapping the two attached petals.

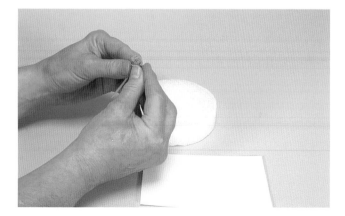

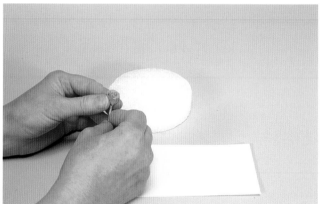

16 Flare the Petal Edge

Flare and shape the third petal. Check to see if the flared petals are similar in height to, or slightly higher than, the top of the prebaked center. If they look uneven, either adjust the flare or peel off the petal and reposition it.

TIP

As long as the clay remains un-baked, you can always make corrections to your rose by peeling off and re-doing the petals. ❧

Making Miniature Flowers With Polymer Clay

Second Layer of Petals

17 Form Balls of Medium Pink Clay

Place the rose in a block of Styrofoam to keep it upright while you work on the next layer of petals. Form three ³⁄₁₆″ (0.5cm) or slightly larger balls (but under ¼″ [0.6cm] in diameter) from the medium shade of pink clay. There are three petals in this layer also.

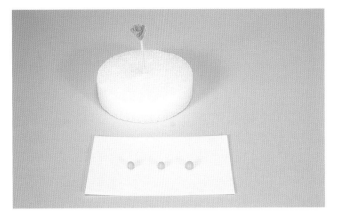

18 Attach the First Petal of the Second Layer

1. Flatten one ball into a round shape, a little wider than the petals in the first layer.
2. Stagger this petal behind the tops of two of the previously attached petals. Press the lower portion of the petal around the base of the first layer.
3. Slightly flare and shape the top of the petal.

19 Attach the Second Petal

1. Flatten and widen the second medium pink ball.
2. Stagger and press this petal behind the next two petals in the first layer, leaving about a third of the space at the side for the third petal to be attached. The petals in the second layer will overlap each other and the bases of the first layer.

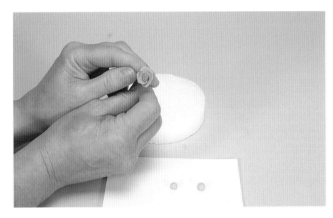

20 Attach the Third Petal

1. Use the third medium pink ball to make another slightly widened petal. Press the bottom of this petal to the base of the rose, filling in the space between the other two petals in the second layer.
2. Flare and shape the petals, keeping in mind that they should be somewhat, but not exactly, even with the tops of the previously applied petals.

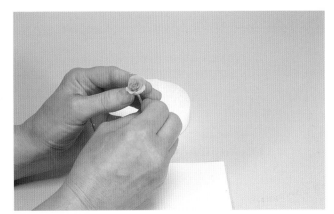

TIP

When attaching the petals, try not to move them down the toothpick or the rose might resemble an artichoke. 🍂

Third Layer of Petals

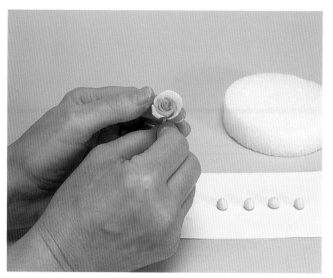

21 Form Balls of Light Pink Clay

Again, place your rose in the styrofoam while you form five ¼″ (0.6cm) balls from the light shade of pink clay. There are five or more petals in this layer.

22 Attach the First Petal of the Third Layer

1. Flatten one light pink ball. Press and attach it, staggering this petal behind two petals in the second layer of petals.
2. Slightly flare the petal's edge.

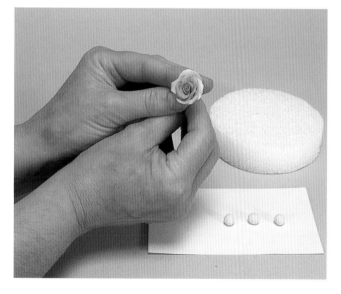

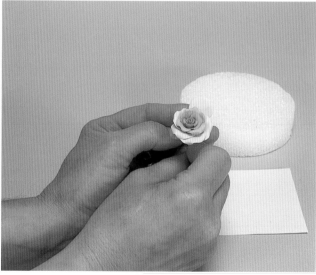

23 Attach the Second Petal

1. The petals in the third, or outermost, row are more overlapped than are those in the inner layers.
2. Press the second petal of this last layer, overlapping much of the first petal.
3. Shape and flare the petal.

24 Continue Attaching Petals

Attach the third, fourth and fifth petals in the third layer, shaping and flaring them as you go.

25 Critique Your Rose

Stop and look at your rose from all angles. Does it look somewhat symmetrical? Does the rose look lopsided? Do the petals need more tweaking? Would your rose look better with another petal or two in the last layer?

26 Add More Petals, if Needed

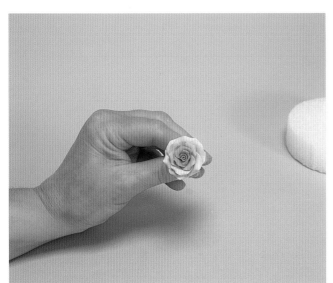

After looking at my rose from all angles, I decided that another two petals were needed in the outer layer. I attached a sixth and seventh petal, which improved the shape and symmetry of the rose.

27 Bake Your Rose

1. Preheat the oven to the temperature recommended by the manufacturer of the clay you are using.
2. Stick the toothpick with the rose attached into a piece of crumpled aluminum foil on a baking pan or cookie sheet.
3. Bake for twenty to thirty minutes as the manufacturer suggests.
4. Remove the rose from the oven and let it cool. It will not be completely hardened until it is cool.

TIP

After baking, smooth out the edges of your petals with an emery board, if necessary. Think of the petal edges as fingernails and you will see where they need smoothing. Don't try to make them too perfect. 🌹

Make a Calyx

A calyx is not always necessary because the back part of the rose might not be seen in some arrangements. The calyx is made from leaf green clay and can be added before baking or after. If a calyx is added to a baked rose, it is best to use a little white glue to hold the calyx in place.

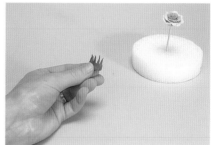

28 Flatten a Teardrop Shape

1. Place your baked rose in the Styrofoam block. Make a ¼″ (0.6cm) diameter ball of leaf green clay. 2. Flatten the ball into a teardrop shape.

29 Cut Five Sepal Shapes

1. Rest the teardrop shape on an index card if it makes it easier to hold it steady. Resting your wrists on a table while cutting can also be helpful.
2. With your cuticle scissors, cut into the point of the flattened teardrop four times. This will give you five pointed sepal shapes. They do not have to be exactly the same size. If they are not pointed, don't be concerned. They can be pinched into points later.
3. Spread the sepal points apart by slightly pivoting and pulling on the sides and base.

30 Wrap the Calyx Around the Base of the Rose

1. If the rose has been previously baked, add a small amount of tacky glue around the base of the rose.
2. Wrap, and stretch if necessary, the base of the calyx around the base of the rose.
3. Position the sepals with a toothpick. Some can be facing downward and some can be pressed up against the sides of the rose. They should look as natural as possible.
4. If some sepal ends are not pointy, press them into a point.

31 Bake the Rose and Calyx

When you are pleased with your calyx, place the rose on the toothpick into a piece of crumpled aluminum foil. (Remember to keep your rose away from the top element of a toaster oven to prevent scorching.) Bake the rose and calyx in the oven according to the directions on your clay package.

Make Rosebuds

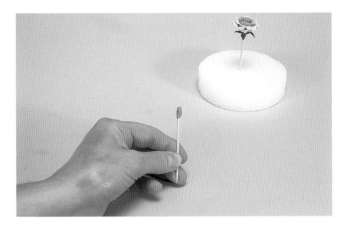

32 Make Rosebuds From Clay

Rosebuds can be either tightly closed or slightly opened. Closed buds are made just like the rose centers. Slightly open buds have one, two or three small petals added. For the buds, it is not necessary to prebake the centers, but if you have some prebaked, all the better.

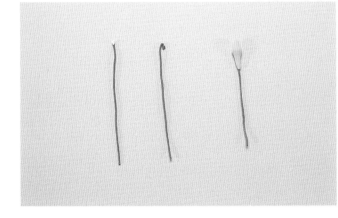

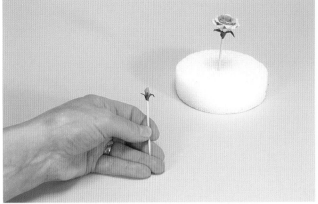

33 Make a Calyx for a Bud

1. Make a smaller version of the rose calyx. If only part of the calyx will be seen, cut only two, three or four sepal shapes into your flattened teardrop shape.
2. Bake the bud with the calyx for twenty to thirty minutes, according to the directions for the clay you are using.

34 Make a Prebaked, Closed Bud

1. Dip the tip of a piece of cloth-covered stem wire into tacky white glue, or make a small bent hook at the tip of the wire.
2. Take a small piece of clay, the color of the roses, and make an elongated teardrop shape. Place it onto the glued stem wire.
3. Bake the bud according to the clay's instructions.

35 Paint the Prebaked Bud

1. Paint the calyx of the bud with green acrylic paint similar in color to the stem wire, as shown. A small amount of burgundy or brown paint can also be painted on the calyx to give a little color variation and interest. Holding the stem on the edge of an index card will help to steady your hand for painting.
2. Paint the tip of the bud with acrylic paint or dry-brush stencil paint, a darker shade of the bud color (in this case, pink), to give it a more realistic look.
3. Remember, if you make a mistake, you can wash off the paint before it is dry and paint it over again!

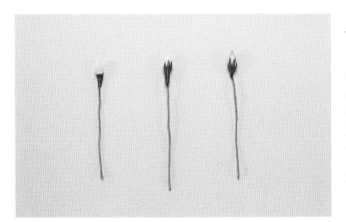

Make Rose Leaves

36 Make a Teardrop Shape

1. Have handy a piece of waxed paper a little larger than your intended leaf.
2. Roll a ³⁄₁₆″ to ¼″ (0.5cm to 0.6cm) ball of leaf green clay.
3. Make a teardrop by rolling the clay on one side of the ball.

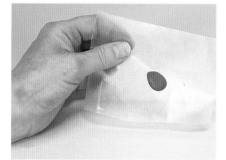

37 Flatten the Teardrop

Flatten the clay teardrop on the waxed paper, rolling the fingertip and pad of your forefinger from the pointed end to the bottom of the leaf. Press the edges thin.

38 Make a Sawtooth Edge

Indent the sawtooth edge by pressing into the thinned edges of the leaf with a fine-toothed comb. Press from the pointed end toward the rounded bottom end on both sides of the leaf.

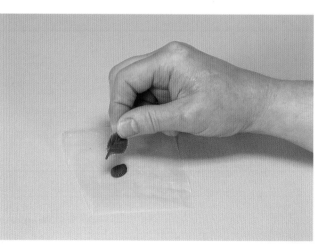

39 Three Ways to Impress Leaf Veins

Here are three easy ways to impress veins in the leaves:
• Press the clay leaf onto a real or plastic leaf, or onto the mold of a leaf. The waxed paper can remain in place. (Cornstarch can be brushed onto the leaf or mold with a dry paintbrush.) The veins of the leaf will be impressed into the clay leaf.
• Press the back of a real or plastic leaf onto the clay leaf while attached to the waxed paper.
• Draw and indent veins into the clay with a straight pin.

40 Make Pointed Leaf Tips Before Baking

1. Pinch leaf tips to make them pointed either by pinching and folding the waxed paper underneath the tip, or by pinching the clay.
2. Bake the leaves either on or off the waxed paper.
3. When cool, paint a few leaf tips with a touch of brown, burgundy or dark green acrylic paint to create a realistic appearance.

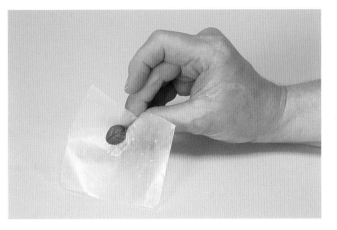

41 Make a Leaf on a Stem

1. Dip the tip of a 3″ (7.6cm) length of no. 26 to no. 30 gauge cloth-covered floral stem wire into white glue. Place it into the Styrofoam block. Make a teardrop shape from a ball of leaf green clay that is ³⁄₁₆″ to ¼″ (0.5cm to 0.6cm) in diameter. Do not flatten the teardrop.
2. Place the broad base of the teardrop onto the glued tip of the stem. Press the base of the teardrop around the end of the stem.
3. Flatten the teardrop between your thumb and forefinger with cornstarch rubbed on them. Or, press the unflattened teardrop onto waxed paper, flattening it from the tip of the leaf to the base with the stem in place.
4. Indent the sides with a fine-toothed comb to create a sawtooth edge.
5. Impress veins onto the leaf.

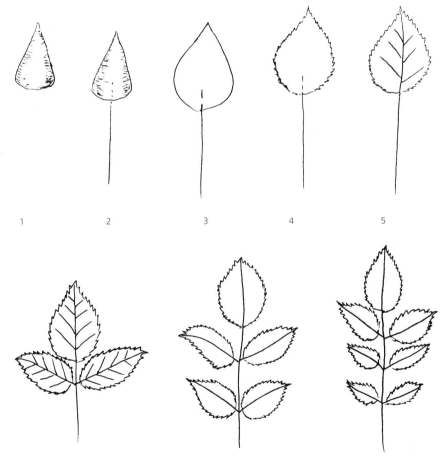

42 Arrange Rose Leaves

Rose leaves are composed of three, five or seven leaflets. Below the topmost leaf, the leaflets occur in pairs, opposite each other on the stem.

TIP

For impressing sawtooth edges on a leaflet, I find that half a comb is better than a whole one because the end teeth of a comb are too stiff. I break a plastic comb in half and, because it is more pliable, use the broken end to make my sawtooth edge. 🌹

43 Attach Rose Leaves to a Flat Surface

Make the top leaflet the largest. For a three-leaflet stem, make the next two opposite leaves smaller. For a five- or seven-leaflet stem, make each pair proportionally smaller than the previous two leaflets. You have a choice of methods for attaching the leaflets:
• Glue all three, five or seven leaflets in proper configuration without a stem.
• Glue all three, five or seven leaflets in place with a cloth-covered stem glued under the top leaf.
• Bake the top leaflet on a stem and glue the additional baked leaflets in place on the flat surface.
• Bake all the leaflets on stems. Then attach them together in the proper configuration with green floral tape, following the directions in step 44.

44 Freestanding Leaves and Stems

1. Bake three, five or seven leaflets on individual stems. Make the top leaflet the largest. For three leaflets, make the next two opposite leaves smaller. If making five or seven leaflets, make them proportionally smaller than the previous two leaflets.
2. Place the largest leaflet at the top and two leaflets opposite one another below the top leaf, as shown.

3. Tape the stems together under the two side leaves with green floral tape to form one main leaf stem.
4. If you wish to place five leaflets on a stem, tape the two smaller leaflets on individual stems opposite each other a short way down the main stem. Do the same with proportionally smaller leaves if you want seven leaflets on a stem.
5. I usually use three leaflets on a stem because the flowers are small.

Finish the Basic Rose

45 Wrap the Freestanding Rose, Rosebud and Leaves

1. Wrap the stem of the rose, the stem of the bud, the three-leaf stem and the five-leaf stem with floral tape that's been cut in half.

2. Then wrap the pretaped stems of the bud and leaves to the rose stem. If the base of the rose stem will be visible, cut it on a diagonal and wrap the tape attractively around the cut. Cut off the excess tape.

REMOVE THE ROSE FROM THE TOOTHPICK

1. The rose can be removed from the toothpick by pushing up on the bottom of the rose center. Don't push too hard on the petals or they might break.
2. If a rose won't budge, cut the toothpick off at the base of the rose.
3. The rose can now be glued in place on your project.

ADD A STEM TO THE ROSE

1. Once the rose has been removed from the toothpick, a stem can be added. For the stem, cut the appropriate length of green cloth-covered floral stem wire. Dip the stem tip into white glue and push it into the hole in the base of the rose left by the toothpick.
2. The floral stem wire can be left as is or can be covered with floral tape.
3. Another option is to glue the toothpick into the rose and then cover the toothpick with floral tape. The disadvantage of this method is that the stem cannot be bent in a realistic way.

46 Finished Basic Rose

The flowers don't always have to be attached to an object. Sometimes they just look attractive placed on or near a favorite knickknack. It makes cleaning easy.

Advanced Roses

In nature, roses abound in a kaleido-scope of colors, shapes and sizes. There are over one thousand varieties that exist at this time. Even on a single rosebush, there is diversity in the flowers. This is a comforting thought, because no matter what my rose looks like, I can tell myself that mine must resemble a real rose out there somewhere. Just as no two roses are exactly alike in nature, each rose that you make will be unique.

The choice is endless, as you'll see through observing roses in nature, florists' bouquets, books, flower catalogs, greeting cards, wrapping paper, calendars, botanical prints, paintings, and porcelain and bone china roses.

The generic basic pink rose that we made is just one way to get started. You have many choices, not only as to color, but also as to the construction of your rose.

A Rose Is a Rose Is a Cup and Saucer

When observing a rose, one way to think of its structure is as a cup and saucer. The illustrations here will give you an idea of this.

Make an Advanced Rose

An advanced rose is one that has more petals and has a more complex center than the basic rose. By following along step-by-step and petal by petal, you will see that there is nothing difficult about modeling them.

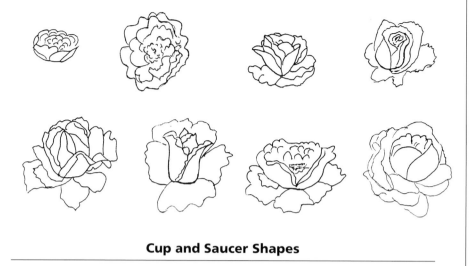

Cup and Saucer Shapes

Some roses are all cup shapes and some are all saucer shapes, like the first two illustrations. Can you see the configurations of the cup and saucer in the other rose drawings? Many roses have this structure.

Direction of the Petals

1. The petals of the cup often stand somewhat straight upward and many are not rolled back at all.
2. The petals of the saucer are often flared and rolled back quite a bit; sometimes the fold is angular. The saucer petals are often positioned somewhat perpendicular to the rose center, and habitually lean downward.

Ten Alternative Rose Centers

There are numerous ways to make rose centers because in nature, roses are so varied. Also, the person modeling the centers might prefer one way of working over another. I hope you enjoy expanding your choices of centers with the following selection.

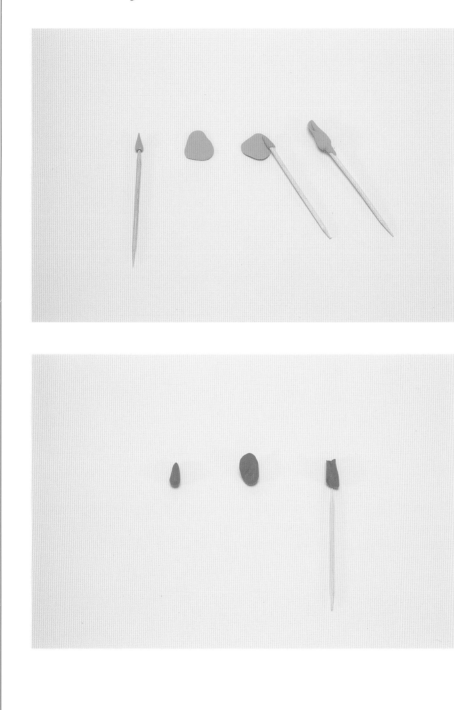

Alternative Center No. 1

1. Make a teardrop shape, place the wide part on a toothpick, bake it and let it cool.
2. Make another unbaked teardrop shape and flatten it.
3. Place the tip of the prebaked teardrop slightly below the tip of the flattened teardrop on the right edge, at the angle shown.
4. Roll from the tips of the prebaked center and the flattened teardrop so that the tip of the prebaked center cannot be seen. (The rolled teardrop is shown a little larger in the photo so that you can see the detail.) It is not necessary to cover the whole prebaked center all the way to the base. Other petals will cover this area. What we are looking for is a pointy center with a slightly unfurling petal.

Alternative Center No. 2

1. Form a teardrop.
2. Pinch the left side of the teardrop and thin with your fingers, leaving part of the thick rounded teardrop shape. Notice that part of the thinned petal is raised higher than the top of the teardrop.
3. Roll left from the teardrop shape onto the petal, wrapping the petal around the teardrop shape, covering the teardrop top. Place on a toothpick and bake at the temperature recommended for your clay.

Alternative Center No. 3

This center is similar to alternative center no. 2, but the center starts with a ball. The ball is thinned into a petal on one side with a rounded teardrop shape on the other side. The thinned part is flattened further, with the side of a toothpick.

1. Form a ball from the clay.
2. Pinch the ball with your fingers to start thinning the petal.
3. Use the side of a toothpick to roll the petal thin. The side of the toothpick also makes the side of the teardrop straight.

Note: The petal top is not much higher than the top of the teardrop.

4. The angle of the toothpick determines the angle of the petal.
5. Roll the top of the teardrop onto the petal. Place the center onto a toothpick.

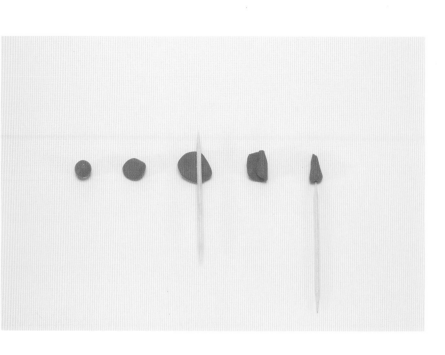

Alternative Center No. 4

1. Press three teardrops flat, and then overlap and press the bases of the petals together.
2. Start rolling left from the top right edge. Keep rolling sideways.
3. Don't flare the petals.
4. Place the base of the center on a toothpick and bake at the temperature recommended for your clay.

Alternative Center No. 5

1. Flatten clay, and cut out a clay shape with a ⅝″ (1.6cm) five-petal Kemper cutter, or a five-petal Friendly cutter.

2. Flatten cutout by first pinching the petals to define and thin them. Then thin the center.

3. Make a tiny hole with a toothpick to mark the center. This will guide you in making even cuts. Cut out the petals as shown.

4. Flatten further, and then start rolling from the right side of the double-petal cutout. Roll onto the next double-petal cutout. Add the single cutout before, or after, adding the second double-petal shape. Notice that I am not flaring the petals backwards, only sideways.

5. Cut out another five-petal shape and follow the procedure of flattening, cutting and adding petals, until you have the center you want. Bake the center at the temperature recommended for your clay.

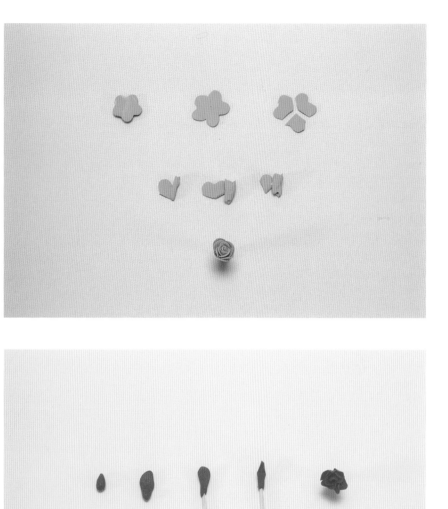

Alternative Center No. 6

1. Make a teardrop shape from the clay.

2. Flatten the pointed end of the teardrop.

3. Place the unflattened end on the toothpick.

4. Push outer edges in toward the center.

5. Add more thin, small petals, with the sides pushed toward the center, until you have about eight or nine petals. Do not flare the petals. Bake the center at the temperature recommended for your clay.

Alternative Center No. 7

1. Use a baked or unbaked teardrop for the center.
2. Make two small, flattened teardrops or circles, then place them on the teardrop tip, opposite one another. They should form a pointed top that covers the tip of the teardrop shape. The pointed top is achieved by rolling the top of the flattened petal with your fingers.
3. Make two more teardrop or circle shapes and place them, opposite one another, where the previously added petals overlapped, or nearly overlapped.
4. Make two more flattened teardrop or circle shapes and press the bases of these over the spot where the previous two petals overlapped, or nearly overlapped.
5. Continue adding petals opposite one another until you are satisfied with your center. Do not flare the petals, and do not roll them tightly at the tops. You want to be able to see the numerous petals.

If you wish, the last two opposite petals' sides can be curved sideways, in opposite directions, to give more movement to the center.

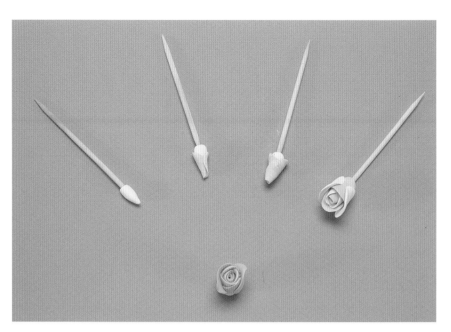

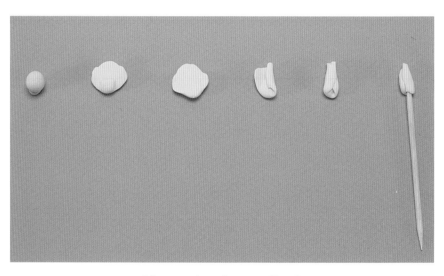

Alternative Center No. 8

1. Make a small clay ball about ¼″ to ⁵⁄₁₆″ (0.6cm to 0.8cm) in diameter.
2. Flatten the tip, sides and a little of the bottom. A bump will remain.
3. Smooth out the side with the smallest bump, turning the remaining bump to the back side. Keep the smoothed side upward.
4. From the top right of the smooth side, roll tightly, from the thinnest part, at an angle toward the thickest part.
5. Wrap the thinned left side around the center.
6. Place on a toothpick. Add more petals before or after baking.

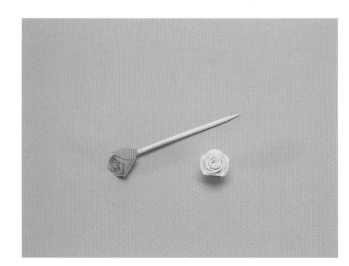

Alternative Center No. 9

1. Make any center core that you like.
2. Keep making tiny balls, flattening them into petals, and adding these petals around the center. Petals get larger as the circumference of the rose center increases. Don't flare the petals.

Bake the center at the temperature recommended for your clay.

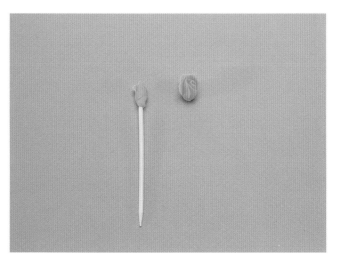

Alternative Center No. 10

1. Make any center core that you like.
2. Add on a petal and bend one side of the petal back.
3. Add and nest other petals that bend back on the same side, producing a spiral effect.

Finish the Advanced Rose

Add the Outer Petals

1. If your center is small, you may wish to add three evenly spaced petals around the center. Then add more petals, as you did in the basic rose.

2. If your center is large, you might just want to add the outer petals in fives, sixes, and so on.

3. You may choose to add the additional petals with two opposite petals, and then add more petals where the first two overlap (or almost overlap) until your rose is finished. Then critique your rose to see if the outer layer needs more petals.

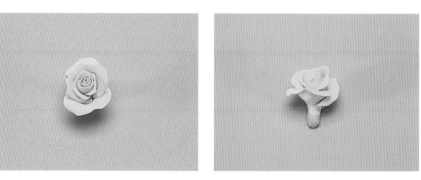

Petal Opposition

1. The yellow rose has only opposite petals outside of the center. Notice that the petals are quite wide, they have substantial overlap, and there is room for some creative curling of the petals.

2. The pink rose has narrower petals; all the petals are opposites, except for the last row, which has five petals evenly spaced around the rose.

Weave Petals Together

1. Do not completely attach the next-to-last petal. Leave the last half, or more, of the petal and the outer edge open.
2. Place the last petal in the open space inside the next-to-last petal.
3. Press the edges together at the base of the rose.

Presentation

Here's a lovely arrangement of multi-hued roses and leaves in a china dish. If you prefer not to add stems, this is a good way to present your finished roses.

Dogwood

Everyone loves dogwood trees for the beauty of their delicate white and pink blossoms, which dot the spring landscape. You can en- joy them throughout the year by making them with polymer clay or other modeling ma- terials. It takes only a few blossoms and leaves to make a branch.

WHAT YOU'LL NEED

- Circle template
- White clay
- Yellow clay
- Leaf green clay
- Cornstarch
- Waxed paper
- Small sandwich bags
- Cuticle scissors
- Sieve or screen
- Pottery clean-up tool or plastic spoon
- Cookie sheet or stoneware plate
- Tacky white glue

- Index cards
- Cloth-covered floral stem wire
- Styrofoam block
- Aluminum foil
- Leaf or leaf mold
- No. 1 round paintbrush
- No. 00 round paintbrush
- Pink and brown acrylic paint
- Paper towel
- Brown floral tape (optional)
- White acrylic paint (optional)

Make Dogwood Centers Without Stems

Prepare the Clay

Soften some white, yellow and green clay by kneading with your hands until it has softened to a workable consistency.

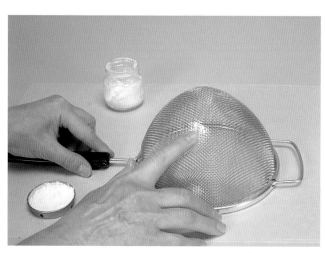

1 Prepare Your Hands and the Sieve

Rub a little cornstarch on the sieve and your hands. You can use a paintbrush to apply the cornstarch to the sieve if you prefer.

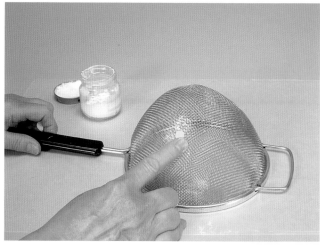

2 Make a Dogwood Center Without a Stem

1. Roll a ball of yellow clay less than ⅛″ (0.3cm) in diameter. If the clay is soft and hard to handle, add a little cornstarch to it.
2. Use your index finger to slightly flatten the ball in the palm of your hand. The clay should stick to your finger.
3. Press the clay onto the sieve to make a pattern on the dogwood center.

3 Remove the Center From the Sieve

1. If the center sticks to your finger, flick it from your finger onto the baking sheet. It's OK if it lands upside down; it can be baked that way.
2. If the center sticks to the sieve, hold the sieve over the baking pan and flick it off with your fingernail or a single-edged razorblade.
3. Bake the centers at the temperature recommended for your clay.

TIP

If, while using a sieve, the holes get filled with clay, press up and down on both sides of the imbedded clay with a ball of clay. The clay ball will pull the clay out of the holes. 🏵

Make a Center on a Stem

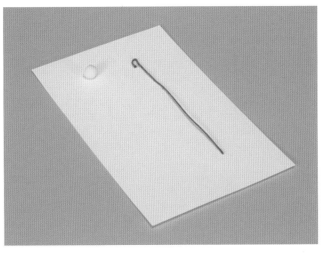

4 Prepare Wire and Clay

1. Dip the tip of a 3″ (7.6cm) length of stem wire into white glue or bend its tip to make a small hook. Set it aside in a Styrofoam block.
2. Make a ball of yellow clay about ⅛″ (0.3cm) in diameter.

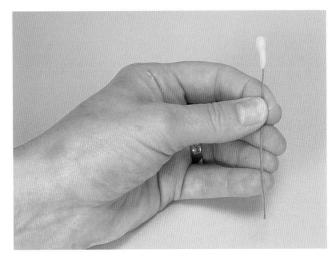

5 Attach the Clay

1. Press the ball of yellow clay over the glue or the hook on the stem wire.
2. Press the lower part of the ball around the stem wire.

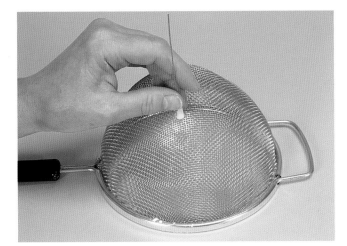

6 Make a Pattern

1. Press the top of the ball into your hand to flatten it slightly.
2. Press the top of the ball onto the sieve to impress the pattern.

7 Bake

1. For baking, place the stem into crumpled aluminum foil. Sometimes it's helpful to first make a hole in the aluminum foil with a toothpick because the stem wires are pliable and might bend rather than puncture the foil.
2. Bake the centers according to the directions on the package of clay you are using.

Make Dogwood Petals

8 Flatten Ball of White Clay

1. Rub cornstarch on a piece of waxed paper approximately 2″ (5.1cm) square. You might want a half index card ready in case you need more surface to work on the petals.

2. Roll out a ball of white clay, from ⁵⁄₁₆″ to ½″ (0.8cm to 1.3cm) in diameter, depending on the size you want your dogwood to be. You can also flatten your clay and cut it to the correct size with Kemper round cutters or a four-petal cutter.

3. Flatten the ball into a circle. The center should be the thickest part.

4. Place the flattened circle on the waxed paper. If it helps to steady your hands when cutting the petals, put the waxed paper and the clay on the half index card for the next step.

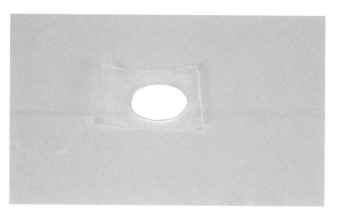

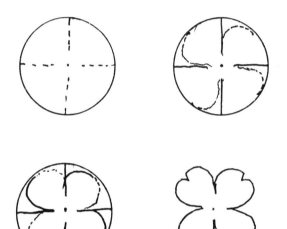

9 Divide the Circle Into Fourths

1. Make a tiny hole in the center of the circle with a toothpick.

2. Cut towards the center of the circle with small scissors, but don't cut the center. Leave approximately ¼″ (0.6cm) of the middle uncut. Dogwood blossoms have four petals and each fourth of the circle will be a petal.

10 Cut Petals From the Fourths

1. Working on waxed paper, slide the blades of your cuticle scissors between the waxed paper and the clay. Make a rounding motion with the scissors to cut the first petal edge.

2. Cut all the way in between the petals to the end of the first cut. Take advantage of the curved edges of the blades. I rotate the waxed paper and cut all the right sides of the petals, and then flip the dogwood blossom over and cut all the right sides of the petals again.

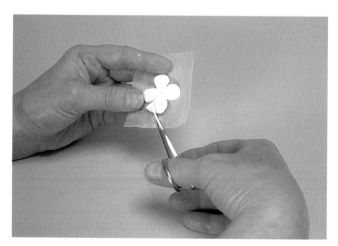

11 Cut Notches Into the Petals

With your cuticle scissors, cut a little *v* shape in the center edge of each petal.

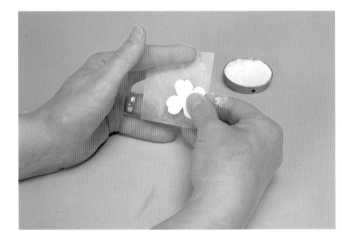

12 Smooth and Round the Edges of the Petals

1. Push the uneven edges in with your fingernail, using the same motion you would use for pushing in a nail cuticle.

2. When the edges are smooth and rounded, lift the blossom off the waxed paper and then put it down again.

13 Separate and Thin the Side Edges of the Petals

With cornstarch on your fingers, pick up the blossom, leaving part of it resting on the waxed paper. Press at the lowest part between two petals to separate them. Use quite a bit of cornstarch to keep the petals from sticking together. Do this with each petal.

14 Separate the *V* Notches

1. Press each petal on either side of a *v* notch and press the *v* open. This also thins the outer edges.
2. Smooth out and round all the edges again.

15 Press in Veins

1. If the original hole is no longer visible, with the tip of a toothpick make another hole in the center of the blossom.
2. Using the curved edge of a ceramic (pottery) cleaning tool, or a small spoon, press curves into each petal by placing the tip of the sculpting tool or spoon into the center hole and pressing in indentation lines. Make five radiating, curved veins on each petal, if possible. The petal veins should radiate from the center hole.

Making Miniature Flowers With Polymer Clay

16 Pinch the Edge at the Notch

Still resting your flower on the waxed paper, pinch each petal together slightly, but not completely, at the *v*, either in an upward or downward pinch. I usually prefer a downward pinch, but both are attractive.

17 Attach Blossom Center

Put a dab of white glue in the center of the dogwood blossom. Press a small, prebaked yellow center in the middle of the flower.

18 Critique and Bake Your Blossom

The dogwood here is natural looking, but sometimes you'll want it to be less flat. You can form flowers into perky shapes by placing objects, such as smoothed aluminum foil, bent index cards, marbles or smooth stones, under the petals to make them uneven. Leave the supporting objects in place until blossoms on the baking surface are thoroughly baked, cooled and hardened.

Make Dogwood Blossoms on Stems

19 Dogwood Blossoms on Stems

1. Put tacky glue around the base of a prebaked center on a stem.
2. With a toothpick, poke a hole through the center of the dogwood and the waxed paper.
3. Poke the stem through the hole in the dogwood and the waxed paper. The waxed paper can remain under the blossom throughout the baking process.
4. The edge of the paper, or extra pieces of folded waxed paper, can be poked up under some of the petals to make them more perky, if you wish.
5. Bake the blossoms according to the instructions for the type of clay you are using.

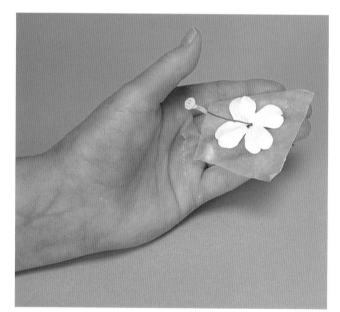

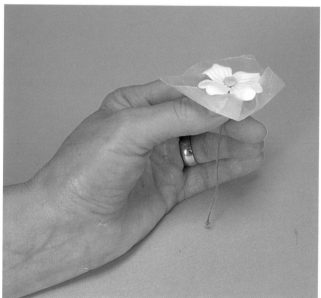

20 Paint the Dogwood Notches With Acrylic Paint

1. Load your no. 1 round brush with pink acrylic paint.

2. Place the tip of the brush underneath the notch and pull a little pink paint up through the notch. If you are not pleased with the effect, you can wipe the paint off with a damp paper towel. I like to paint all the pink notches at once.

3. When the pink paint has dried, load a no. 00 round brush with some brown acrylic paint and place the tip of the brush under the notch. Pull up a little brown paint, leaving some of the pink paint visible.

21 Make Dogwood Leaves

Dogwood leaves are made the same way rose leaves are, except they don't have a sawtooth edge. See pages 40-41.

TIP

If I want to tone down the color, a wash of white paint can be painted over the notches. A little lime green paint and/or brown paint can be painted on the centers' surfaces if you wish. 🍂

Arrange Blossoms and Leaves

You can simply glue the unstemmed blossoms and leaves to the surface of your project. To set at different levels or to place some flower petals under others, glue height adjuster slices under the flowers or glue the blossoms onto leaves.

Floral tape

1

2

3

Arranging Leaves and Blossoms on Single Branches

You'll need brown floral tape (cut in half the long way), five dogwood blossoms on stems and ten dogwood leaves on stems.

1. Wrap the stems of two leaves together with the floral tape. Continue wrapping two leaf stems together until you have five sets of double leaves on stems.

2. Wrap each blossom's stem with the halved brown floral tape.

3. Tape a dogwood blossom stem onto a double-leaf stem a short way down the stem from the leaves. Tape each blossom on a double-leaf stem in the same way.

4. Using one combined blossom/ leaves stem as a base, attach, with the halved brown floral tape, another of the dogwood blossom/leaves stems, leaving some of the second stem showing. When attached securely, cut off the excess stem of the second blossom/leaves combination.

5. A little further down on the first stem, attach a third blossom/leaves stem. Leave the excess tape-covered stem wire.

6. Use one of the last two blossom/ leaves stems as another base. Attach the remaining stem below the base dogwood blossoms. Leave the excess stem.

You now have two separate dogwood branches, one with three dogwood blossoms and attached leaves, and another with two dogwood blossoms and attached leaves.

The branches can be placed in a container arrangement as they are or they can be attached, as shown in the next step.

Attaching the Branches

7. Place the two branches next to each other, staggering the blossoms. Decide on the length you want for the branch. Tape the branches together at the base. Cut off the excess stems on a diagonal. If the base of the branch will be visible, attach the tape in a neat way around the diagonal to give the look of a finished branch that has been cut on the diagonal. The diagonally cut end of the branches can either come from the top right or left, or the bottom right or left when you are mounting the branches in a picture or on an object. Glue the branch in place on the object or place it into an arrangement.

H O W   T O   M A K E

Daisies

A daisy is made from a flat round piece of clay. The number of petals can vary from eight to sixteen, depending on your preference. If a doublepetaled daisy is required, place a second flat round of petals over the first, staggering the petals, if possible. The petals on top should be made from a slightly smaller circle.

WHAT YOU'LL NEED

- White clay
- Yellow clay
- Leaf green clay
- Cloth-covered floral stem wire, approximately no. 24 gauge
- Needle-nosed pliers
- Sieve or screen
- Aluminum foil
- Toothpicks
- Circle template
- Tape
- Waxed paper
- Paper punch, ⅛″ (0.3cm)
- Index cards
- Cornstarch
- Kemper cutter, ¾″ (1.9cm) round
- Cuticle scissors
- Single-edged razorblade
- Tacky white glue
- 5/16″-½″ (0.8cm-1.3cm) 5-petal cutter

Make Daisy Centers and Petals

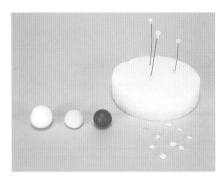

1 Knead the Clay and Make the Centers

1. Knead white clay and yellow clay.
2. You can mix a little white in with the yellow for different shades. Flowers look more realistic if the colors are not all the same.
3. Make the prebaked centers, either on or off a stem, following the instructions for the dogwood centers on pages 54-55.

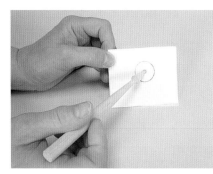

4 Cover the Work Surface With Waxed Paper

Tape waxed paper over the work surface. With a tool, poke a hole into the waxed paper through the center hole. Put cornstarch on the card surface around the punched hole.

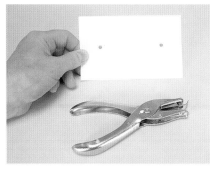

2 Create a Work Surface

1. You need three index cards and a ⅛″ (0.3cm) paper punch. Stack the cards. Using the paper punch, punch a hole through the cards.
2. Repeat the punch on the other end of the stack.

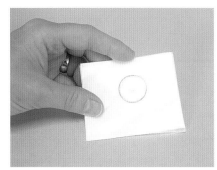

5 Make a ¾″ (1.9cm) Flattened Circle

1. Flatten a piece of white clay. Make it quite thin.
2. With a Kemper ¾″ (1.9cm) round cutter, cut a circle from the clay—or just flatten a ball with your fingers into a ¾″ (1.9cm) round of clay.
3. Press the clay circle into the hole in the work surface.
4. Press the center of your clay circle into the center of the punched-out hole.

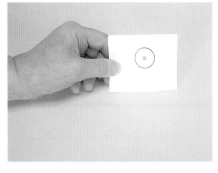

3 Cut and Glue

1. Cut the cards in half.
2. With tacky glue, glue three of the halves together so the holes are aligned. Glue the other three halves onto this stack with all the holes matching.
3. You have six thicknesses of half index cards with a hole in the middle. Rotate a toothpick in the hole to make sure the holes are lined up.
4. With the circle template, trace a circle ⅞″ (2.2cm) in diameter, keeping the punched holes on the stacked and glued index cards in the center of the circle.

6 Secure the Center of the Cutout on the Reverse Side of the Work Surface

You can add more white clay to the underside of the hole and push it into the interior to help secure the top cutout. Poke a small indentation into the center of the circle with a toothpick.

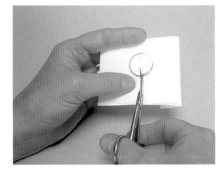

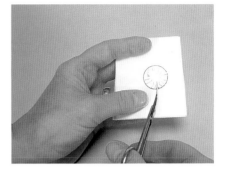

7 Divide the Circle

1. With a single-edged razorblade, gently raise the flattened clay outside of the center. Add more cornstarch under the clay. Do this all around so only the center sticks to the card. The blades of cuticle scissors should slide under the clay easily.

2. Cut into the circle towards the center leaving ¼″ (0.6cm) uncut in the center. Periodically snip your scissors through cornstarch and continue to cut each half until the circle is divided into fourths.

8 Make Eight or Sixteen Sections

Cut each fourth in half, making eighths. Leave ¼″ (0.6cm) in the center. You can stop here or make sixteen petals.

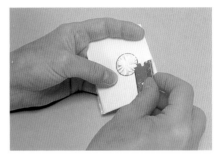

9 Make Pointed Tips

1. Cut in around the sections. Start at the center edge of a petal and cut toward the middle of the daisy, leaving the ¼″ (0.6cm) center uncut. Do this on both sides of the petals, pointing the center of the petal edge.

2. Periodically snip your scissors through the cornstarch.

3. You may have to reposition some sections with a single-edged razorblade to cut them out. The petals don't have to be the same size.

10 Indent the Petal With a Toothpick

Again, for this step it's easier not to go in order. Dip the side of a round toothpick into cornstarch. Press each petal from the center hole to the edge of the petal. Use a single-edged razorblade to lift some of the shaped petals to make room for the last petals to be shaped.

11 Glue the Center and Bake

Slice the daisy off the card work surface onto a baking sheet and glue on your prebaked center.

A Daisy With a Stem

12 Attach the Prebaked Center on a Stem

1. Place some glue around the base of the prebaked center on a stem.
2. Push the stem with the center through the center of the daisy and the hole in the index card work surface.
3. Pinch the clay underneath around the stem, and push the daisy on the stem up and out of the hole. You might have to add more clay at the bottom.
4. If your daisy is floppy, place the stem through a small piece of waxed paper and leave it under the daisy to hold the petals in place while you make the calyx.

13 Make a Calyx

Knead a piece of leaf green clay. Flatten it. Cut a five-petal shape with a ⁵⁄₁₆″-½″ (0.8cm-1.3cm) Kemper five-petal cutter. Pinch the petal edges into points, making a star shape. Another option is to use needle-nosed pliers to point the tips of the petals on the cutter so it becomes a star shape.

14 Attach the Calyx

1. Press the calyx lightly onto the center hole of the index card work surface or onto a small piece of waxed paper.
2. Poke the daisy on the stem through the center of the star shape on the work surface or the waxed paper. Press the daisy and calyx together slightly.
3. If the daisy sticks to the waxed paper on the work surface, cut the paper off the work surface. If you used a small piece of waxed paper alone, it can just stay in place during the baking.

15 Critique and Bake

1. Look again at the daisy. Do the petals need staggering or would they look more natural if some of the petals were turned left or right, or nudged up or down? Would it look more real if a petal or two were pinched together at the tip? Does it look perky? The waxed paper can be folded and bent to act as a prop for the petals.
2. Poke a hole into the crumpled aluminum foil with a toothpick. Place your stem into the hole in the aluminum foil. Bend the stem almost in half if you are using a toaster oven, so that it will not hit the oven top or scorch from being too near the element.
3. Bake for twenty to thirty minutes.
4. Cool the stems and daisies in the aluminum foil. To restraighten the wires, fold back in the opposite direction from the bend.
5. Petals can be cut, rounded and separated with the small curved scissors after baking.

Variation: Make a Stronger Daisy

1

Make a flat, thin round of clay, about one-third smaller than the circle on your work surface. Press the round onto the work surface with the punched hole in the center.

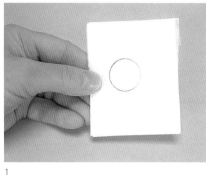

1

2

Make a thin coil of white clay. Thin the end of the coil. Press the tip of a toothpick over the thinned end to make a petal.

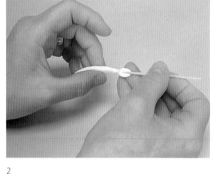 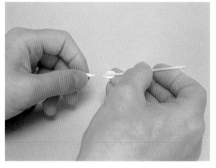

2   3

3

Pinch the rest of the coil off with the fingers of your other hand.

4

Keeping the petal attached to the toothpick, press the petal onto the center of the round of clay on the work surface. Line up the edge of the petal so it is even with the edge of the circle that was traced on the work surface. You will end up with a uniformly round daisy.

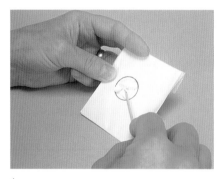 

     5

5

Continue making and adding petals in opposite halves, fourths, eighths, etc., until the daisy has all the petals it needs.

6

Glue on a prebaked center with tacky glue.

6

TIP

If petals get knocked off, don't worry. Make a small thin coil, tapered at the top. Press down onto the index card and press in center groove with toothpick. Put a tiny amount of white glue on the broken petal with a toothpick and press the new petal onto it. Bake twenty minutes. You might make a circle of unbaked petals to have in reserve. Baked petals can also be glued on.

Make Daisy Leaves

1 Begin the Leaf

1. Make a flattened, leaf green teardrop of clay, with or without a stem. (See Make Rose Leaves.)
2. Thin around the edges and then place the clay onto a waxed paper or index card surface.
3. Press the leaf down onto the surface and use a T-pin to indent a center vein.
4. Cut into the sides of the leaf with three or four shallow, straight or angled slits. Do this on both sides of the leaf's perimeter.

2 Make Pointed Edges

1. Using a craft knife, cut a sharp tip from the inside edges of the slits toward the leaf's tip. I find it easiest if the tip of the leaf faces toward me. With the tip of the craft knife, remove the excess clay.
2. From the inside of the next slit to the edge of the previously worked slit cut out a *v* or triangle, making a sharply toothed, uneven edge.
3. Repeat on both sides of the leaf, moving from slit to slit until you have pointed edges on the leaf.
4. With the T-pin, press side veins in from the center vein out to the pointed tip on each side of the leaf.

Cherry Blossoms

W e live in the Virginia suburbs of Washington, DC. Several years ago, my husband and I went to the Cherry Blossom Festival. I wanted to see the beautiful Yoshino Cherry Blossoms and decide if I could possibly make similar blossoms from clay. The following cherry blossoms are a result of that trip.

WHAT YOU'LL NEED

- Light pink clay
- Leaf green clay
- White thread
- Yellow-green thread
- Plastic drinking straw
- Tacky white glue
- Needle-nosed pliers (optional)
- Cloth-covered floral stem wire (approximately no. 26 gauge)
- Acrylic paint: brown, yellow-green, green (similar to the stem wire), burgundy, dark pink (darker than the clay), dark green, optional (darker than the leaves)

- Dry-brush stencil paint: dark pink, optional (darker than the clay)
- Stencil brush or eye shadow applicator (optional)
- Extender or water
- Styrofoam block
- Water-based varnish (optional)
- T-pin or other pin
- Index cards
- Waxed paper
- Kemper ⅝″ or ¾″ (1.6cm or 1.9cm) five-petal cutter
- Single-edged razorblade
- Generic leaf for veining

- Fine-toothed comb
- Toothpicks
- Cuticle scissors
- Scissors
- Cornstarch
- Paintbrush
- Brown floral tape

Make the Blossom Centers

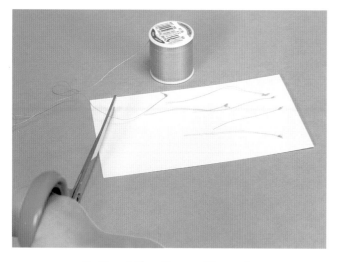

1 Knot the Green Threads

Cut several 1½″ (3.8cm) lengths of yellow-green thread and make knots at one end. It is easier to knot each length of thread before cutting it off the spool.

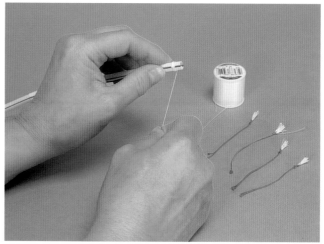

2 Wind the Thread Around the Stem Wire and Straw

Place a 3″ (7.6cm) piece of stem wire on one side of a drinking straw. Hold it against the side of the drinking straw with one hand. Wind white thread around the straw about sixteen times, encircling the stem wire as well.

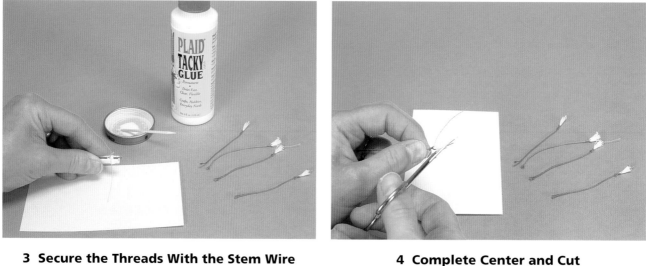

3 Secure the Threads With the Stem Wire

Place a dab of tacky white glue on the thread at a point where it's on top of the stem wire. Place one of the 1½″ (3.8cm) green threads on the glue with the knot hanging over the edge.

4 Complete Center and Cut

Hook the tip of the wire over the threads to clamp them together. Press and wind the wire together with your fingers or needle-nosed pliers. Leave the stem wire in place. Remove the straw and cut the white thread loop in half. Do not cut the green thread. You now have a cherry blossom center.

Finish the Centers

5 Paint the Centers

Spread the threads apart and paint the tips of the white threads with brown acrylic paint. Let the paint dry. You can use the center as it is. Just spread out the threads. I prefer to go a step further and varnish the threads.

6 Glue the Threads Together

Look at the center from the top. Place a little tacky glue on the top of the green wire and press the threads together to conceal the wire and to form the threads into a circular center. While the glue is wet, pull the longer green thread up through the white threads to the middle. Let dry.

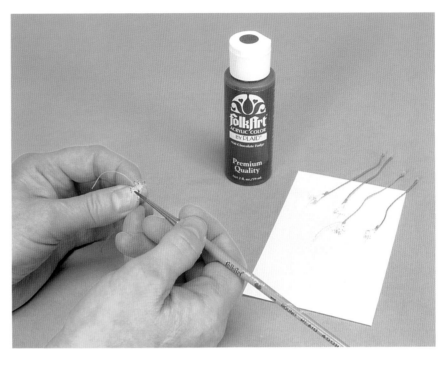

STEPS TO STIFFEN AND WATERPROOF CENTERS

1. Dip the thread center into water-based varnish.
2. Press some of the varnish back into the varnish container.
3. Working quickly, with a T-pin near the base, spread threads apart with a back and forth motion using the side of the T-pin. Keep separating the threads at the base; they will spread.
4. Pull the T-pin up between the threads that are sticking together. I must confess that I look through an embroidery magnifying glass in order to see to do this.
5. Poke the stem end into your Styrofoam block. Let it dry.

Cut the Cherry Blossom

7 Prepare the Clay

Knead some light pink clay. Flatten the clay to about 1/16″ (0.2cm), keeping the center a little thicker.

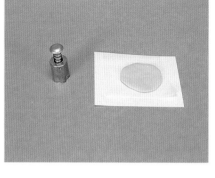

8 Cut the Shape

Cut out a pink five-petal shape using a ⅝″ or ¾″ (1.6cm or 1.9cm) Kemper five-petal cutter.

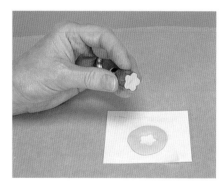

9 Make the Hole

Place the pink shape onto waxed paper or an index card. Make a tiny hole with a toothpick or your cuticle scissors in the center of the flower.

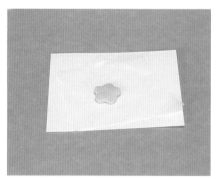

Making Miniature Flowers With Polymer Clay

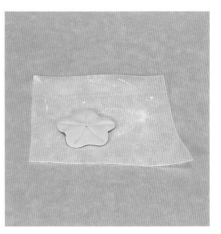

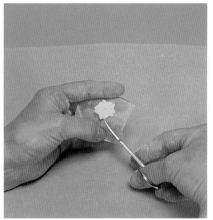

10 Pinch

Pinch the top surface and underside of each petal to define and thin. Place onto an index card or waxed paper.

11 Center Hole and Indentations

If the original hole has closed up, make a tiny hole in the center of the cutout. Make indentations from the center hole to the center edge of each petal.

12 Form *V*

Cut a tiny *v* shape, in the tip of each petal near the indentation. Pinch the petals over the *v*-shaped notches to separate them. Rest most of the petal on the waxed paper or index card.

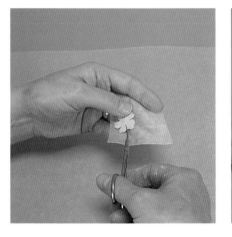

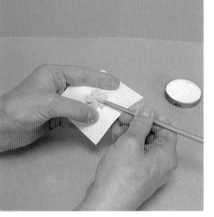

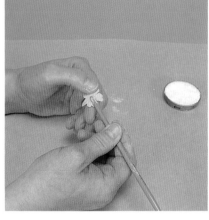

13

With the center hole as a guide, use cuticle scissors to cut between each petal, separating and narrowing. Leave about ¼" (0.6cm) uncut in the middle. Press between the petals to separate and thin the edges between them.

14

1. Work on the waxed paper or index card or over the side of your index finger rubbed with cornstarch. Press the side edges of one petal with a paintbrush handle dipped in cornstarch. Then thin the rest of the petal on each side of the *v*.
2. Press the petal's top edges toward the *v* as you finish each.

Attach Blossoms to the Stems

15

1. Put tacky white glue around the stem center and place it in the Styrofoam block.
2. Poke a toothpick through the waxed paper through the original hole in the center.

16

1. Push the stem through the hole and waxed paper. Squeeze the opening at the base of the threads closed around the center.
2. Squeeze and shape the clay base around the stem, but leave most of the thread center showing.

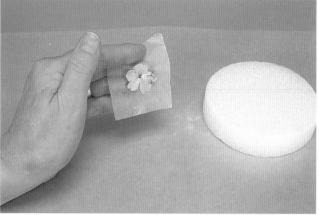

17

1. Add softened, pink clay to the stem underneath the blossom, forming an elongated calyx. This will be painted green after baking. If the blossoms will be put in a frame, don't make the calyxes too long for the depth of the frame.
2. Twirl where the petals and the calyx meet so they blend together.
3. Bake your cherry blossoms for twenty to thirty minutes at the temperature suggested by the manufacturer of the clay.

TIP

Set aside your blossoms if the clay is too soft or the petals are floppy. Place the stems in Styrofoam with the flower heads bent downward. When they are colder and firmer, transfer the stemmed flowers to crumpled aluminum foil for baking. Sometimes it helps to put a piece of waxed paper or a smooth piece of aluminum foil under the blossom to hold it in place.

Paint the Blossoms and Calyx

18

1. Thin yellow-green acrylic paint with extender or water.
2. Use a paintbrush to brush a tiny amount of paint near the bottom of the center threads, near the base and between the petal bottoms.
3. You may wish to get some pale green on the base of the threads.

19

1. Paint the calyx under the blossom bottom with a green similar to the color of the stem wire.
2. Start at the lower part of the calyx on the stem and paint up. Paint in the arches between the petals with the green. Accent the lower part of the calyx with burgundy and use it on some of the calyx tips.
3. Paint a bit of yellow-green near the base and between the petals right above the calyx arch. You can leave your cherry blossom as it is or add more shading.

20 Add Shading

There are two methods for shading the blossom. For each, your brush must be dry.
• Leave the middle of the flower natural pink. Paint over the edges and toward the center sparingly with a darker pink dry-brush stencil paint using a stencil brush or an eye shadow applicator.
• Follow the above directions, but dry brush the blossom using darker pink acrylic paint with extender or thickener added. Paint with a small flat brush.

Make the Buds and Leaves

21 Making the Buds

The buds are similar to rosebuds but the tips are more rounded. Glue the buds to 3″ (7.6cm) lengths of stem wire. Darken the tip of the bud with the darker pink you used for shading your cherry blossom.

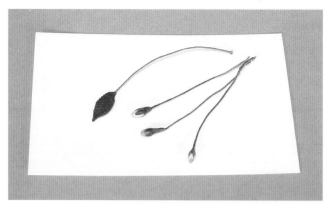

22 Making the Leaves

1. Use leaf green clay to make a slightly long teardrop shape. Don't flatten it.
2. Press the wide part of the teardrop around the stem so it's also pointed.
3. Make sawtooth edges around the cherry blossom leaf similar to the edge on the rose leaf.
4. Vein with a real leaf or a generic leaf mold. Using a leaf larger than your clay leaf lets you see where the center vein is in relation to the tip and center of your leaf.
5. Paint some leaf tips with burgundy or a darker green for more interest.

Arrange Cherry Blossoms on Branches

For One Branch

1. Begin with five leaves, three cherry blossoms and three buds all on stems for one branch.
2. Make a whorl of the five leaves. Tape the stems together with brown floral tape that has been cut in half the long way.
3. Hold the stems of one blossom and two buds together. Using the half-width brown floral tape, tape the blossom and two buds to the stem with the leaves. Tape them together in one place a little way down from the whorl of leaves. Don't cover the whole length of the green stems with brown tape—a portion of the green stems should show.
4. Tape two more blossoms and one bud to the same branch. Place these blossoms and bud onto the leaf whorl stem near the end. If you want to add another branch, the second branch's blossoms should fit between those on the first stem.

Combine Two Branches

1. Tape two blossoms and two buds together with half-width brown floral tape to make a second branch.
2. Tape the two branches together at the ends, positioning the blossoms of the second branch between the blossoms of the first branch. Cut the branch ends on a diagonal and tape the base together. The diagonal at the base of the branch gives the branch a finished look.
3. The branch can be turned with the diagonal end at the top or the bottom for framing. I usually place the diagonally cut branch base at the top right or left of a picture if I am framing it.

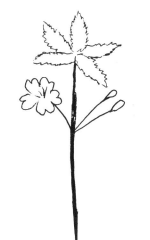

Branch 1

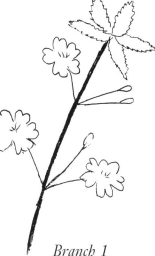

Branch 1

Branch 2

Combined Branches

H O W T O M A K E A
Pansy

P ansies are dainty, co-lorful and informal, with their sweet impish faces and prolific blooms. They appear in exciting color combintions that enchant me and invite me to try, however impossible, to create clay clones that mimic the form and color of each individual beauty.

WHAT YOU'LL NEED

- Purple clay
- White clay
- Yellow clay
- Leaf green clay
- Index cards
- Circle template
- Kemper cutter, $\frac{7}{16}''$ (1.1cm) heart shape
- Kemper $\frac{3}{8}''$ or $\frac{7}{16}''$ (1.0cm or 1.1cm) five-petal cutter
- White crepe paper
- Rolling pin or brayer (optional)
- Cornstarch
- Single-edged razorblade
- Pottery clean-up tool

- Baking pan
- Waxed paper
- Part of a wide-toothed comb
- Veined leaf facsimile
- No. 0 or no. 00 size liner brush
- Water
- Acrylic paints: white, yellow and purple and/or black
- Dry-brush stencil paint: a darker shade than pansy petals
- Stencil brush or eye shadow applicator
- Fine-tipped black permanent marker or pen
- Box, optional (greeting card box or top of shoe box)

Make Pansy Centers and Petals

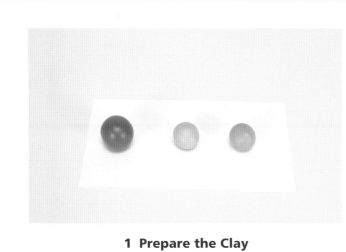

1 Prepare the Clay

1. Knead a 1″ (2.5cm) ball of purple clay and add a ¼″ (0.6cm) ball of white. This makes a dark purple.
2. Knead a 1″ (2.5cm) ball of purple clay and add a 1″ (2.5cm) ball of white clay making a lighter purple clay.
3. Knead a ½″ (1.3cm) ball of green clay and ½″ (1.3cm) ball of yellow clay together, making a yellow-green for the pansy centers.

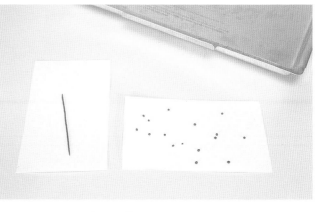

2 Make Yellow-Green Centers

1. Roll a coil, about the thickness of thin spaghetti, from the yellow-green clay.
2. Pull off a small end of the coil, rolling it between your fingers into a ball, and let the tiny ball drop onto a baking pan. The balls should be small enough to fit inside the triangle of your pansy.
3. While you're at it, you might as well make several centers.
4. Bake the centers for twenty minutes at the temperature recommended for the type of clay you are using.

3 Cut Dark Purple Petals

1. Flatten the clay to slightly less than ⅛″ (0.3cm).
2. Using a ⁷⁄₁₆″ (1.1cm) Kemper cutter in a heart shape, cut two dark purple hearts.

4 Cut Light Purple Petals

1. Flatten light purple clay to less than ⅛″ (0.3cm) thick.
2. Using the same Kemper cutter, cut out four light purple shapes. If you don't have a cutter, make six balls approximately ⁵⁄₁₆″ (0.8cm) in diameter.

5 Cut a Base to Construct the Pansy On

Using the ⅜″ or ⁷⁄₁₆″ (1.0cm or 1.1cm) five-petal cutter, cut out a light purple shape.

6 Make a Guide and Work Surface

1. Use a circle template and a fine-tipped permanent ink pen to trace a circle ⅞″ (2.2cm) in diameter approximately in the center of an index card. You can also use an index card that's cut in half the short way. I prefer a half card because my hands are small. You'll construct your pansy on this card.
2. Press the five-petal shape onto the lower middle portion of the circle on your index card so it's almost like a miniature pansy, with two petals at the top, one petal on each side and one petal at the bottom of the shape.

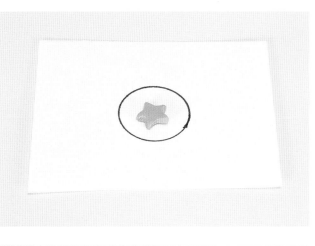

7 Make the Top and Side Petals

1. With a little cornstarch on your fingers, squeeze the two top lobes of the heart together to eliminate the indentation. Press on either side of this point and then press on the point to widen the petal. Keep a pointed bottom on the petal.
3. Press around the edges to thin.
4. Do the same with the next three petals. The top petals are dark purple and the side petals are light purple.

8 Make Veins in the Petals

There are two methods to vein the petals:
• Vein the petals with white crepe paper.
1. With scissors, cut a piece of white crepe paper about 9″ (22.9cm) long and 2″ (5.1cm) wide. Follow the direction of the unstretchy grain for the length.
• Thin and vein the petals with the side of the toothpick.
2. Press one flattened petal on the crepe paper so the lines on the paper go from the top to the bottom of your petal.

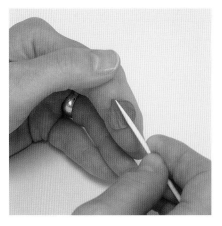

TIP

Cutting the crepe paper into a long strip acts as a reminder that the veins should go up and down. You won't have to stare at the crepe paper to see which direction the lines are going. Use white crepe paper because some of the other colors may not be colorfast and might discolor your clay. 🌸

Attach Pansy Petals

9 Attach the Upper Left Petal

Press the pointed end of a veined, dark purple pansy petal onto the upper left petal of the cutout on the index card.

10 Attach the Upper Right Petal

Vein the next dark purple petal. Bend the left side of this petal up a little. Place the pointed end on the upper right point of the cutout, slightly overlapping the two petals where the second petal is bent.

11 Attach the Right Side Petal

Vein a light purple petal. Turn it so the bottom pointed end is in the center and on the right side.

12 Attach the Left Side Petal

Vein another light purple petal. Turn it so the bottom pointed end is in the center and on the left side.

Notice that part of the five-petal cutout base is still visible below the side petals. If it isn't, attach another little piece of flattened light purple clay under the center of the petals. To do this, lift the lower part of the flower with a single-edged razorblade. Press down slightly on the base of the petals, being careful not to press down the top edges of the petals.

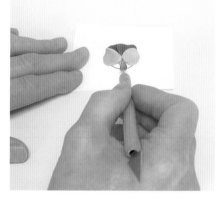

13 Make the Triangle Center

1. Press the lower edge of the side petals together where they join.
2. Use the curved side of a pottery clean-up tool and press a triangle between the two side petals near their base. The triangle shouldn't go to the top where the petals join.
3. Leave all pieces attached to the card.

Paint the Pansy

14 Paint the Side Petals

1. Pour a dab of black or purple acrylic paint onto another index card.

2. Dip your brush into water and then roll it on the side of the dab of paint. You need to thin the paint to an ink consistency. Roll your brush on the card to make the ends come to a point.

3. Working from the right edge of the triangle towards the center of the right petal, brush wispy strokes, lifting the brush tip as you get close to the center of the petal.

4. Continue making wispy strokes until you are satisfied with the basic shape of the face. If it needs darkening, fill in the inside of the face with more black or purple, but don't go over the wisps. If you do, you might lose the delicate, natural look.

5. Repeat with the left petal, stroking your brush from the left edge of the triangle toward the center of the petal. Let the paint dry.

15 Paint the Triangle

1. Squeeze a dab of white acrylic paint onto your index card palette. Roll your brush on the side of the dab of white paint. Don't thin the paint this time.

2. Paint the top sides of the triangle white. It's OK if white gets into the triangle center. Let the paint dry.

Make the Front Skirt Petal

16 Front Skirt

1. Place the last two heart shapes next to each other so the lobes are on the bottom and the pointed ends are next to each other on the top. Press them together so that you have a shape with four curves at the bottom.

2. Press each curve with your fingertips to thin and define the shape. Press around the edges so you create a shape similar to the one pictured. It looks sort of like butterfly wings.

3. Vein with the crepe paper from top to bottom and set aside.

17 Attach the Front Skirt Petal

1. Place the center of the straight top across the middle of the white triangle.

2. Press the center of the petal into the triangle with a sculpting tool or toothpick. Be careful to leave the triangle of white edges intact.

TIP

For a variation of the front skirt petal, place one heart on top of the other. This front petal will have one indentation in the center. Pinch up around the petal to widen it. Sometimes the petal has to be shortened, either at the top or the bottom. Use scissors to do this. Then press the edges thin again.

Paint a Face on the Skirt

18 Paint the Face on the Skirt

1. Roll your brush in inky black or purple acrylic paint just as before.
2. Start slightly below the triangle and paint a face on the skirt.

19 Paint the Yellow Center

1. Squeeze a dab of yellow acrylic paint onto your index card palette. Roll the brush at the edge of the dab to load with paint.
2. Place the tip of the brush inside the triangle and paint from the top to slightly over the bottom edge onto the petal, making a rounded shape. Be careful not to paint over the white edges. Set aside to dry.

Here are some samples of faces. Remember to keep the edges wispy!

Finish the Pansy

20 Drop in Center

1. Place the pansy into a shallow box, like a stationery box or a shoe box top.
2. Drop a center into the triangle. If you miss, try again. The box will keep the green centers from rolling out of sight.
3. Press the prebaked center into the triangle with a toothpick, so it and the unbaked clay bond during baking.

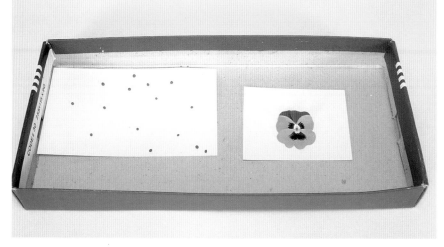

21 Critique and Bake Your Pansy

1. Look to see if the petals need some centering or perking up. Sometimes a toothpick works better than your fingers.
2. You might want to raise the top left petal edge slightly.
3. Check to make sure the left edge of the right top petal is raised off the left petal.
4. The top of the right petal should be raised from the back petal.
5. Make sure the left petal is raised from the back petal.
6. The skirt top should be raised from the side petals.
7. Sometimes the bottom of the skirt needs pinching together at the hemline center.
8. Sometimes the skirt is too long and needs shortening at the bottom with a pair of scissors. Thin the edges again.
9. Bake the pansy on the card for about twenty to thirty minutes following the directions for your particular type of clay.

Making Miniature Flowers With Polymer Clay

Make the Leaves

1 Make Indentations

Pansy leaves are similar to rose leaves except: the top of the leaf is rounded and the perimeter has indentations. Use a comb with widely spaced teeth to make the indentations.

2 Vein the Leaves

Use a real, plastic or jewelry leaf, or make a mold with similar veins. The veining in a celery leaf is similar to the veining in a real pansy leaf.

3 Pinch the Leaf Tip Together

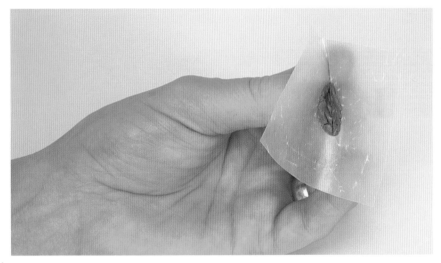

Here are some examples of veining for pansies.

HOW TO MAKE

Daffodils

Daffodils, the bright harbingers of spring, are a welcome sight after the gray of winter. We have a row of them along the edge of our suburban woods, and these lovely bulbs light up the landscape in a brilliant yellow glow.

WHAT YOU'LL NEED

- Yellow clay
- White clay
- Leaf green clay
- Transparent clay
- Terra-cotta clay
- Cloth-covered floral stem wire
- Wooden clay tool, ³⁄₁₆″ to ¼″ (0.5cm to 0.6cm) in diameter, rounded at one end with a dull point at the opposite end, or a pencil with a clean rounded eraser on one end and a dull sharpened point at the other end (cover the lead with tape or clay)
- Index cards
- Rolling pin or brayer
- Cornstarch
- Craft knife (optional)
- Toothpicks
- Pin, T-pin or needle tool
- Aluminum foil
- Circle template
- Cuticle scissors
- Scissors
- Acrylic paint: orange, lime green or leaf green
- Lime green floral tape
- Flat paint brush, no. 2
- Extender or water
- Waxed paper
- Tacky white glue

Make Daffodil Centers

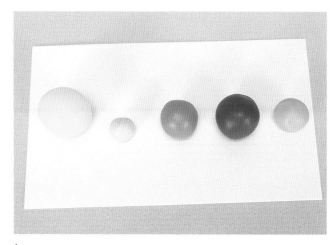

1 Prepare the Clay

1. Knead a 2″ (5.1cm) ball of yellow clay mixed with a ½″ (1.3cm) ball of white clay to make a light yellow.
2. Knead the leaf green clay.
3. Mix some yellow.
4. Mix together some transparent clay with a tiny piece of terra-cotta clay.

2

Dip the tip of a 3″ (7.6cm) length of cloth-covered floral stem wire into tacky white glue.

3

Make a tiny ball from your yellow/white/green clay mixture. Place the ball on the glue on the stem wire.

4

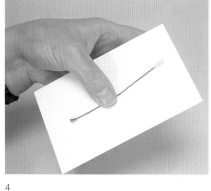

Work the clay down the stem wire.

5

Flatten the top slightly. Press in with a pin on three sides to form a shape that looks something like the one shown here. Bake for fifteen minutes at the temperature recommended for the type of clay you are using.

Making Miniature Flowers With Polymer Clay

Form the Daffodil Trumpet

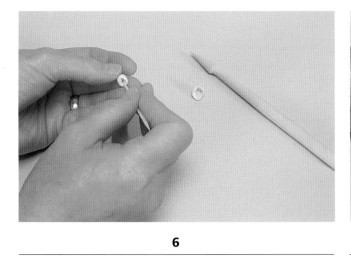

6

1. Roll a ball of the yellow clay ¼″ to ⅜″ (0.6cm to 1.0cm) in diameter. Use a circle template to measure it.
2. Hollow out the center with a toothpick.

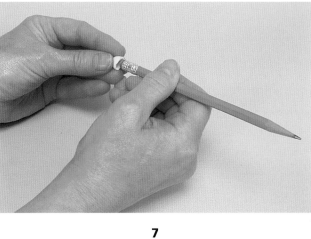

7

1. Press the rounded end of a clay tool or round pencil eraser in and out of the trumpet.
2. Thin and ruffle the sides and top of the trumpet with the toothpick.

8

1. Put the rounded end of the clay tool or pencil eraser into the trumpet to reshape it.
2. Press the top of the trumpet close to the shaft of the tool. Round and flatten the bottom of the trumpet.

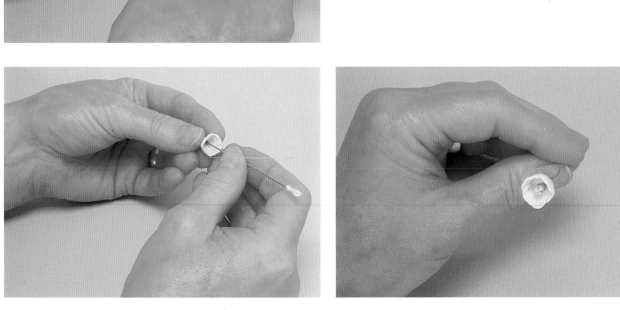

9 Join the Trumpet and Center

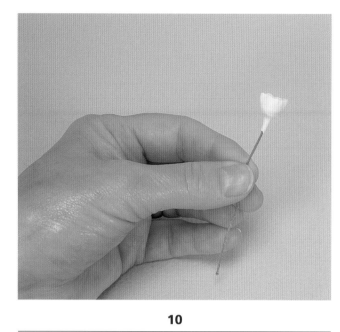

10

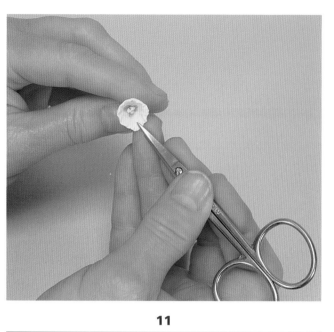

11

Form some of the yellow clay down the stem from the bottom of the trumpet or add a little more yellow clay around the base of the trumpet. This will be painted green later for a calyx.

1. Use cuticle scissors to push the top edge down slightly so it curves outward. Press the trumpet in a little, under the outward curving edge.
2. Bake fifteen minutes at the temperature recommended for the clay that you are using.

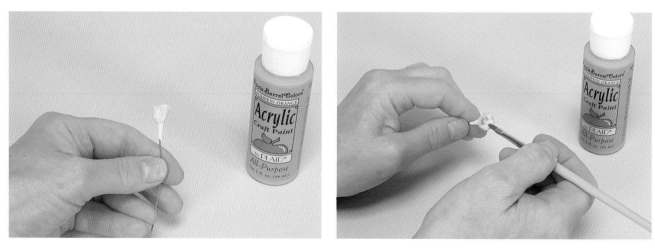

12 Paint the Baked Trumpet

Paint the trumpet with acrylic orange paint using a no. 2 flat brush with some extender or water. Let the yellow shine through toward the base of the trumpet. Paint the top edge of the trumpet darkest.

Make the Daffodil Petals

13 Make a Template

1. Trace a six-petal template onto waxed paper or tracing paper. Cut it out with scissors.
2. Make an index card template of the six-petal shape by tracing around the waxed paper cutout. Cut out two or three, while you are at it. You will use these index card templates to cut out the six-petal shapes.

14 Flatten Clay and Position Template

1. Use your fingers to flatten a ball of yellow clay about the same size as the template.
2. Rub a little cornstarch onto the top and bottom of the clay.
3. Place the clay onto the piece of waxed paper and press the template onto the flattened clay circle.
4. Use cuticle scissors or a craft knife to cut around the petals of the template.
5. Gently pull the template off the clay.
6. Look at the clay petals' back and front and use the best side for the right side of your petals.

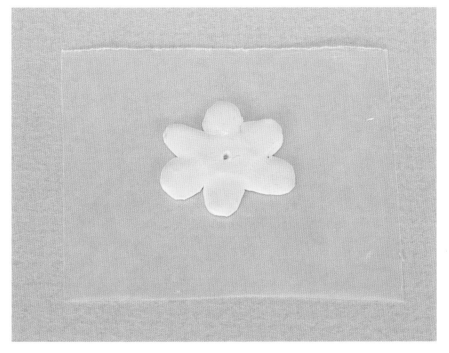

15 Thin and Define the Petals

1. Pinch the lobe of each petal to define and thin.
2. Place the cutout back onto the waxed paper on the index cards.
3. Make a tiny hole in the center of the cutout with cuticle scissors or a toothpick. For an easy daffodil, you might not need to cut in any more.

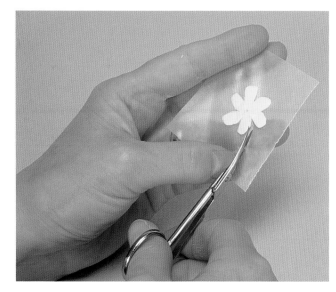

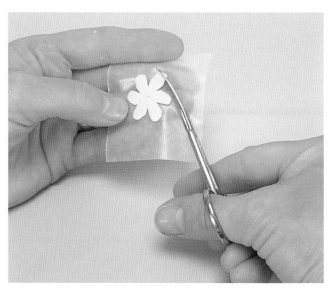

16 Cut, Separate and Narrow Petals

1. Cut in toward the center hole to separate and narrow the petals.
2. Lift the petals off the waxed paper and put them down again on the waxed paper.

17 Critique Your Petals

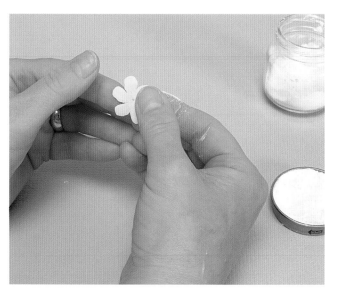

1. Look at the petals. Are they about the same size? Are there irregular angles? Round the edges. Think about the petals as fingernail edges. Are they smooth or angular? You can press the cutout down onto the card and use your fingernail to shape the petals.
2. One of my petals was too long. I'm cutting it down here.

18 Press With Cornstarch to Separate and Thin

Separate and thin the petals by putting some cornstarch on your fingers and then lifting some of the petals and pressing between them. Or, you can just keep the petals on the waxed paper and thin the edges down.

19 Indent the Petals With Paintbrush Handle

Shape the petals with the end of a smooth paintbrush handle or a toothpick that has been dipped into cornstarch.

Pinch the center edge of each petal upward at the tips. Tweak the petals to make them look perky.

21 Attach the Trumpet

1. Poke a T-pin, or similar tool, in the center holes of the petals and through the waxed paper.
2. Put a little glue on the base of the trumpet and push it through the hole. Shape the petals.
3. If the calyx doesn't show, add more yellow around the bottom and taper it down on the stem wire.

Paint the Calyx and Make the Sheath

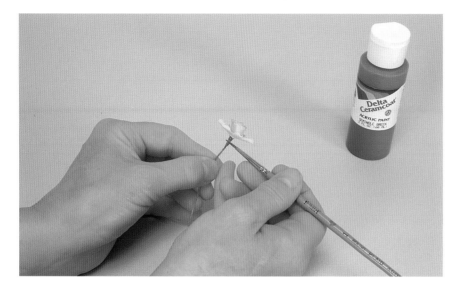

22 Paint the Calyx

Use yellow-green or leaf green paint that matches the color of the floral tape. Let the paint dry.

23 Bend the Stem of the Daffodil

Decide which way the daffodil looks best when it's bent forward and bend it at the lower end of the calyx.

24 Make the Sheath and Bake

Make a small teardrop of the transparent/terra-cotta mixture. Press to make the top end pointed and then press both sides of the lower end to flatten and thin the teardrop. Place the flattened teardrop on the lower part of the calyx with the pointed end up and the rest of the sheath tapering down to the size of the stem wire. Make sure no stem wire shows between the calyx and the sheath. Place the sheath low so the stem can be easily wrapped with the floral tape without damaging the petals of the daffodil. Bake for twenty to thirty minutes at the temperature suggested by manufacturer. After baking, tape the stems with green or lime green floral tape.

Making Miniature Flowers With Polymer Clay

Daffodil Buds and Leaves

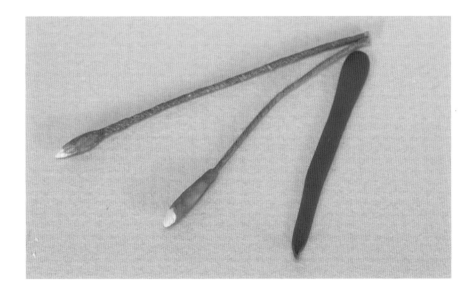

Make Daffodil Buds and Leaves

For the Buds:
1. Roll a small ball of yellow clay.
2. Dip the stem wire into tacky glue.
3. Press the clay onto the wire, tapering it down the stem and pointing the tip.
4. Bake the bud.
5. Paint the lower part of the bud green.
6. Cover the stem wire with the same color floral tape that you used on the daffodil stem.

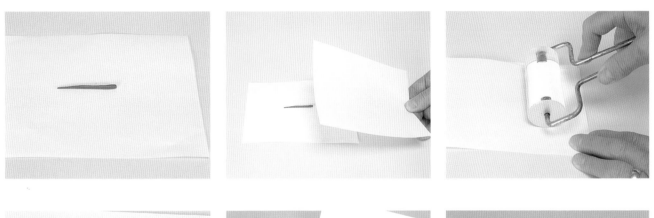

For the Leaves:
1. Make a thin coil about 1½″ (3.8cm), or a little shorter, on an index card.
2. Point the tip.
3. Cover the coil with a piece of waxed paper or another index card.
4. Roll over the covered coil with a rolling pin or brayer.
5. Remove the card. Pinch the tips and turn them to look natural. Some can even be draped over foil or another material to make the leaves bend realistically.
6. Several leaves can be pressed together at their bases and then baked. Extra baked leaves can be added to fill out the design.

Irises

The iris inspired Louis VII of France to embrace the fleur-de-Louis, now known as the fleur-de-lis, as his symbol. This seems a logical choice since this regal flower is resplendent in royal purples as well as luxurious golds. Contrarily, the iris is also called the poor man's orchid. To me, the abundance of the iris signifies our good fortune, rather than suggesting this flower is ordinary. The precious iris is available to people of every economic circumstance. With plenty of irises available, over two hundred varieties, we can find many subjects to inspire us to try our hand at making them from polymer clay.

WHAT YOU'LL NEED

- Purple clay
- White clay
- Leaf green clay
- Yellow clay
- Acrylic paint: yellow, white and brown
- Index cards
- Waxed paper
- Cuticle scissors or craft knife

- Styrofoam
- Brayer or rolling pin
- Cloth-covered floral stem wire
- A penny
- Tracing paper (optional)
- Lime green floral tape
- Cornstarch
- Single-edged razorblade
- Aluminum foil

Make the Iris Center

Prepare Your Clay

For the petals, mix purple with a little white. Mix leaf green, yellow and white to make a yellow-green that matches the color of the florists' tape you use. Lime green tape works well with irises.

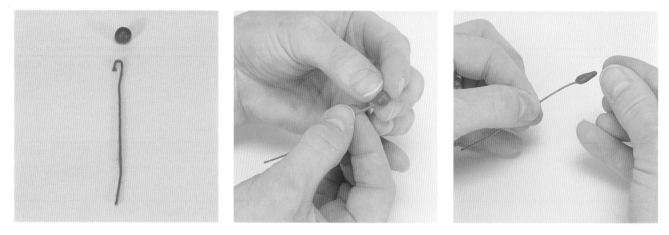

1 How to Make Irises

2 Form a Teardrop With a Point

1. Make a small ball of purple clay ⅛" (0.3cm) or less in diameter.
2. Dip the tip of a stem wire in tacky glue or make a small hook on the tip of the stem.

1. Press the ball onto the stem. Shape the top into a point and press the base around the stem, forming a teardrop shape.
2. If the teardrop shape is too big or long, just pull the end off and repoint it.

3 Cut Into the Point of the Teardrop

1. With cuticle scissors, snip into the point to make three tiny petals. To do this, cut into the tip once then cut the thickest part again. In other words, make one snip, roll it over, holding it by the stem, and give the largest remaining point another snip.
2. It's easiest if you hold the stem sideways on a half index card or hold the teardrop against your finger to steady your hands. Holding your elbows close to your body also helps to steady your hands.
3. The tiny petals don't have to be even and it's not a problem if green from the stem wire shows. Don't worry if you cut the top wrong, just repoint it and cut again.
4. Bake the centers for twenty minutes at the temperature recommended for the brand of clay you are using.

Make the Top Petals

4 Make a Template

1. Make a three-lobed pattern and trace over it with a piece of waxed paper. Cut out the pattern on the waxed paper with scissors.
2. Trace around the waxed paper cutout onto an index card.
3. The index card pattern is your template. Cut it out. You may wish to make more than one template for future use while you are cutting.
4. You'll use the same template for the top and bottom petals.

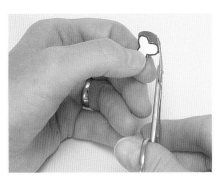

5 Cut the Three-Petal Clay Shape

1. Flatten a circle of clay about the same size as the index card template. Put a little cornstarch on the top and the bottom.
2. Place the template on the clay circle.
3. With your craft knife or cuticle scissors, cut around the pattern to form the petals. It's easiest if your clay is close to the size of the template and you just need to cut between the petals. Round the petals with your finger before removing the template.
4. Remove the template and place the clay cutout onto waxed paper with cornstarch on it.

TIP

If you are cutting clay using a template and a craft knife and too much clay stretches out from under the template, use a chopping, up-and-down movement with the side of the knife rather than gliding the tip of the knife around the template. The edges can be smoothed later. ❧

6 Flatten and Thin
the Iris Petals

1. Put some cornstarch on your fingers.
2. Start at the outer edge of each lobe and flatten each petal in two or three pressing motions.
3. Press the petal cutout lightly onto waxed paper or an index card to further define the petals if needed.

7 Make the Raised Center Vein on Each Petal

1. Make a tiny hole in the center of the cutout with a toothpick tip.
2. Make a raised center vein on each petal by pressing the side of the toothpick from the center hole to a spot on the petal's outer tip next to the center. Repeat on the other side of the center, leaving a small raised line. The edges of the petals on either side of the line are thick, but we'll thin them later.

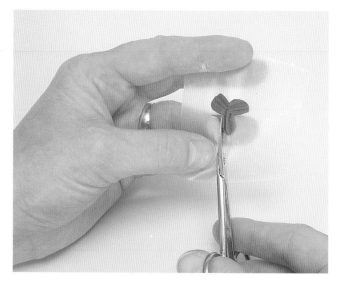

8 Cut Between the Petals

Cut each petal deeper into the center to separate them. If necessary, adjust the size of the petals.

9 Thin and Indent the Petals' Edges With a Penny

1. Use the edge of a penny with an upward/outward angle to make markings on each petal.
2. I find it easiest to start at the base of each petal. Push in lightly on the edge angling toward, but not all the way up to, the raised center line.
3. Mark the other side of the petal with your penny by turning the waxed paper over so you can work from the top down. Look at the petals. Turn them so you can see where you are indenting with the penny edge.
4. Leave the petals on the waxed paper after they're marked and pinch upward at the tip of each petal.

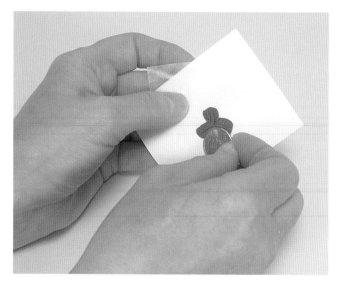

Making Miniature Flowers With Polymer Clay

Attach the Center

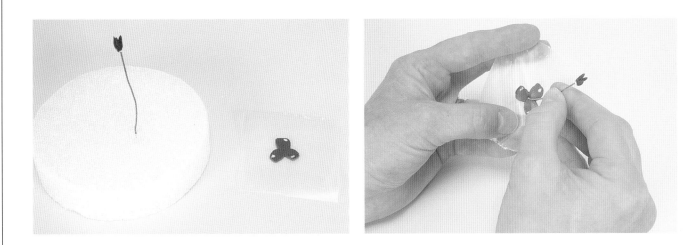

10 Attach the Prebaked Center on the Stem to the Cutout

1. Dab tacky white glue around the base of the prebaked centers.
2. Turn the unbaked petals so that the underside is up.
3. Put a tiny dab of glue near the edge of every other petal if you want a closed top.
4. Still working on the waxed paper, poke a hole through the center of the petals and the waxed paper.
5. Put the stem through the petals and the waxed paper.

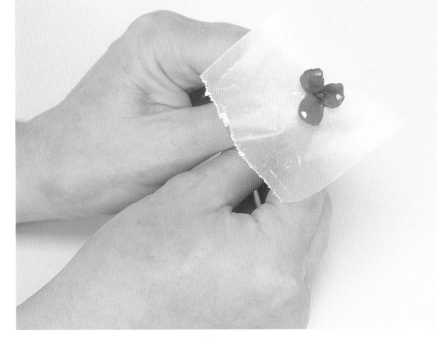

11 Finish and Bake

Push the petals up. Pinch the petals together where the glue is. The waxed paper can stay in place. Bake the iris' top petals for twenty minutes at the temperature suggested for the type of clay you are using.

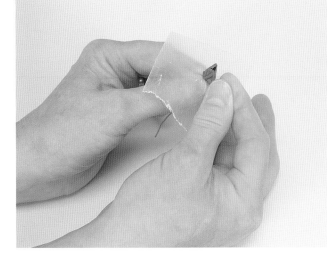

Make the Bottom Petals

12 Use the Three-Petal Template

1. Place the same template onto a piece of flattened clay, slightly thicker than the thickness you used for the top petals. This will make the bottom petals a little larger.
2. Follow the same procedure that you used for the top petals, but let the ends of the petals extend a little beyond the edge of the template. Don't pinch the edges of the petals together as you did with the top. Leave the waxed paper under the petals as you work.
3. Make a hole in the center of the bottom petals through the waxed paper.

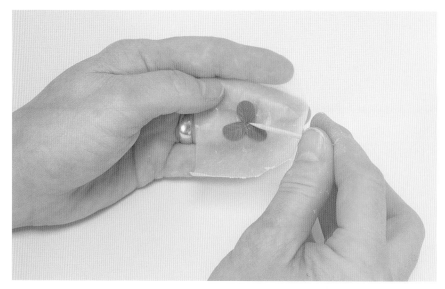

13 Glue the Prebaked Top and the Unbaked Bottom Petals Together

1. Put a dab of white glue under the base of the prebaked top. Set it into a Styrofoam block.
2. Lift the bottom petals off the waxed paper. Place them over the hole in the waxed paper with the top, veined side up.
3. Put the end of the stem through the hole and attach the bottom petals to the prebaked top.

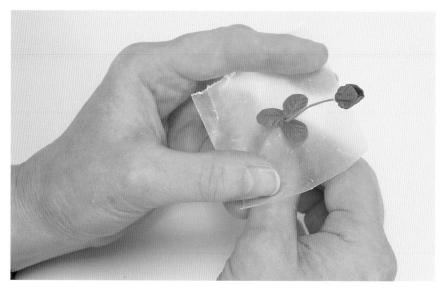

14

Stagger the top and bottom petals. Leave the petals on the waxed paper.

15 Make the Calyx Base

1. Make a small ball of lime or yellow-green clay by mixing leaf green, yellow, and white.
2. Remove the waxed paper from under the bottom petals.
3. Place the ball of lime green clay around the stem under the bottom petals. Elongate the green part so that it ends below the petal bottoms when they're bent downward. You need to wrap the florists' tape on the stem below the petals so they won't break.

16 Bend and Bake

Bend the petals down, as shown here. Bake the iris according to the directions on the clay's package.

17 Paint the Iris

Use a very thin, round paintbrush, to paint the veins on the three bottom petals yellow. Paint from the center out, but not all the way to the edge.

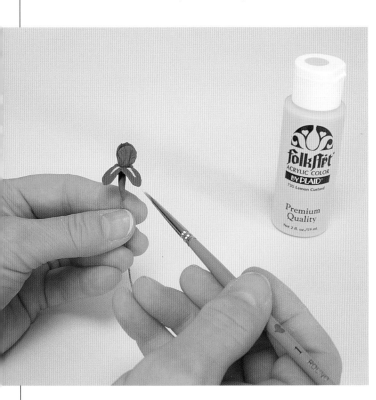

TIP

If you are painting an iris with a yellow fall, you may need to add a little orange on the top of the petals' center veins. ❧

Make the Iris Bud

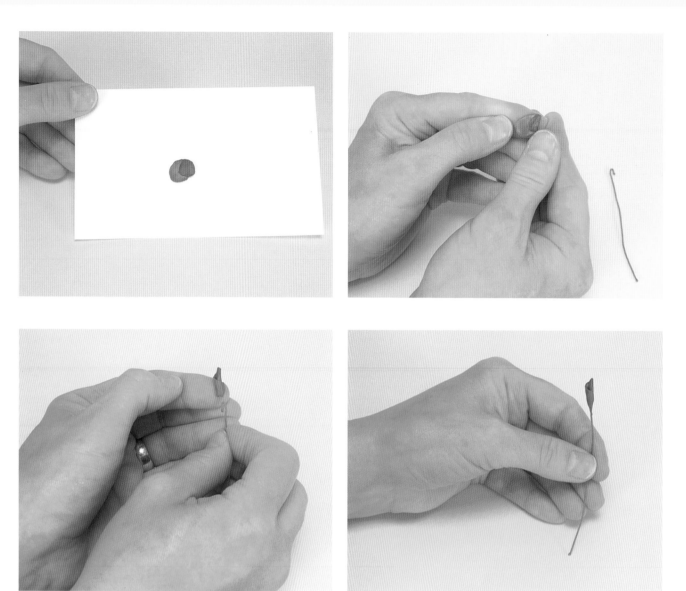

18

1. Make a green teardrop shape and flatten it.
2. Make a small flattened teardrop shape the color of the iris petals.
3. Press the small flattened teardrop of purple clay with the pointed end extending above the pointed part of the flattened green teardrop. (At this point, it is probably not pointed but that's alright.)

4. Press the two parts together.
5. Starting at the top, roll inward.
6. Dip a stem into some tacky white glue. Poke the bud onto the stem.
7. Bake for thirty minutes at the temperature recommended.

Make the Iris Leaves

19

1. Make a thin coil about 1½″ (3.8cm) or a little shorter on an index card.

2. Point the tip.

3. Cover the coil with a piece of waxed paper or another index card.

4. Roll over the covered coil with a rolling pin or brayer.

5. Remove the card or paper. Pinch the tips and turn them to look natural. Some can even be draped over foil or another material to make the leaves bend realistically.

6. Several leaves can be pressed together at their bases and then baked. Extra baked leaves can be added to fill out the design when you are assembling your project.

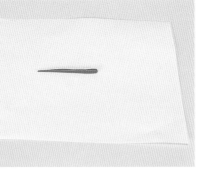
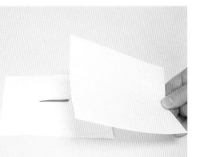
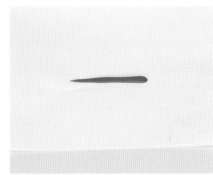

PRESENTATION &
Project Ideas

Polymer clay flowers can adorn surfaces made of almost any material, such as wood, glass, crystal, china, silver, brass, copper, terra-cotta and pottery. Inexpensive surfaces can be made to look expensive and elegant by enhancing them with polymer clay flowers. The flowers make great jewelry, too!

Framed Projects

Arranging polymer clay flowers in picture frames is an excellent way to display your work and to enhance your room decor. Frames without glass can be used to create charming three-dimensional pictures. Shadow box frames with glass inserts are excellent for exhibiting your floral sculptures since they have the depth required to encase the flowers. When protected by glass, flowers of exquisite delicacy can be safely displayed.

All of these are suitable choices for framed arrangements.

WHAT YOU'LL NEED

- One open rose without a stem
- One or two rosebuds
- Ten rose leaves
- A small brass photo frame (2½″ to 3″ [6.4cm to 7.6cm])
- Off-white moiré fabric, about the size of the frame
- Cardboard, the size of the frame
- Tacky white glue
- Scissors
- Toothpicks
- Spray adhesive

Project: Rose in a Small Frame

This simple framed arrangement is a good first project and is great for small, inexpensive gifts and decorations. The design can be adapted to display many of the individual flowers in this book.

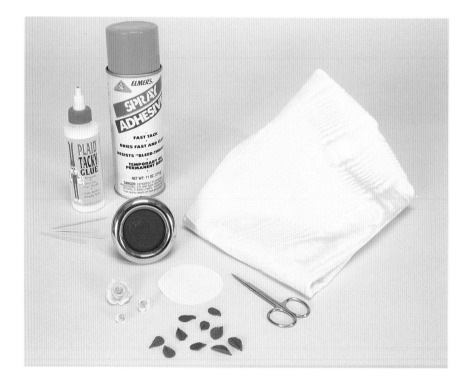

1 Assemble Your Supplies

Making Miniature Flowers With Polymer Clay

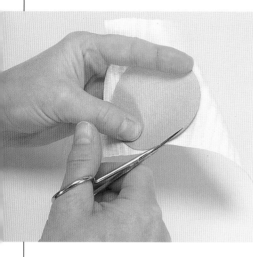  

2 Prepare the Frame

1. Remove any glass and backing from the frame.
2. Cut a piece of cardboard that will fit inside the frame.
3. Using the cardboard as a template, cut out a piece of moiré (fabric) the same size.

4. Glue the wrong side of the fabric to the cardboard with spray adhesive.
5. Place the fabric-covered cardboard into the frame and replace the backing.

3 Attach Flowers

1. Glue the open rose to the center of the framed background fabric with the tacky white glue.
2. Arrange the buds and leaves attractively under and around the rose. Using a toothpick and tacky white glue, affix the buds and leaves to the backing material. Try to apply the glue so that it does not seep out from under the objects.

Stand back and admire your handiwork!

Project: Roses in a Shadow Box Frame

This project is an easy, but well-balanced design, and is suitable for many of the flowers we've made in this book.

You might want to choose your shadow box frame and double mat before making your flowers. A double mat gives an elegant, finished appearance to your arrangement.

A 5″×7″ (12.7cm×17.8cm) frame is standard size, so pre-cut double mats can be purchased to fit inside. This is less costly than having mats cut to fit your frame. The pre-cut mats are equally attractive as custom-cut mats and there is a wide variety of colors available.

If you can't find a matching color, combinations of white and off-white are subtle and compatible with most flowers and home decor styles. Of course, you have the choice of using custom-made frames and mats.

- Three open roses without stems
- Two or more rosebuds, some on thin cloth-covered wire stems
- Fifteen rose leaves
- A shadow box frame, 5″×7″ (12.7cm×17.8cm)
- Pre-cut double mat
- Cardboard, a little smaller than the size of the frame
- Off-white moiré or other fabric
- Tacky white glue
- Scissors
- Toothpicks
- Spray adhesive
- Window cleaner
- Masking tape or other tape
- Sawtooth hangers and nails
- Glaziers' points (available at hardware stores) or small nails
- Hammer
- Wallpaper or craft paper, about the size of the frame

TIP

When using spray adhesive, I usually put the items to be sprayed into a large cardboard box to spray them so the spray is contained. 🌹

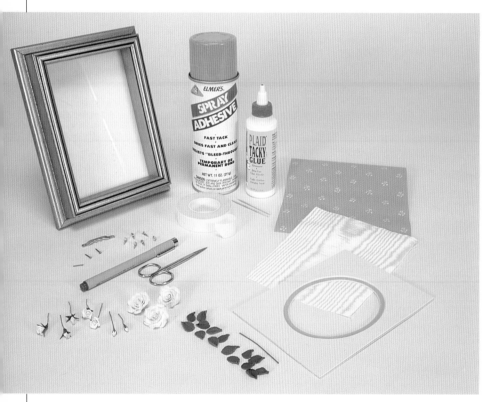

1 Assemble Your Supplies

2 Prepare Your Background

1. Cut a piece of cardboard a little smaller than the mat. Often the frame itself or the pre-cut mat will have a cardboard backing that can be used. A scrap piece of acid-free mat board is also an excellent choice because it might prolong the life of the fabric covering.
2. Cut the moiré or other fabric to fit the cardboard backing.
3. Glue the fabric to the cardboard with spray adhesive.
4. Turn your mat so that the wrong side is up. Center it on top of the moiré-covered board. Lightly tape it to the cardboard. By using an upside-down mat, you don't have to worry about getting glue on the good side and the mat will act as a guide to help you center your design.

3 Compose the Arrangement

Arrange the roses, buds and leaves as shown. Glue the design onto the fabric with tacky white glue, and let it dry for twenty-four hours before framing.

4 Sign Your Name

Since you have hand sculpted and arranged these flowers, sign your name on the mat at the lower right of the opening. Writing on the mat is easier than writing on the fabric. I use a thin Micron Pigma pen in brown.

5 Attach the Mat to the Arrangement

1. Place the opening of the mat over your arrangement. Check to see if the design looks centered. There should be a little room to move the cardboard inside the mat opening to get it centered. When the design is positioned to your satisfaction, tape the arrangement to the back of the mat with masking tape.
2. Place your arrangement in the frame. Use glaziers' points, nails or tape to secure your project into the frame.

Jewelry and Ornaments

Wonderful and unusually beautiful jewelry can be created with miniature polymer clay flowers. The capability of duplicating the color of almost any flower and fabric is an advantage when matching flower jewelry to your clothing. Polymer clay flower jewelry looks equally appropriate on tailored business suits, gossamer dresses, denim shirts and evening wear. The clay is light in weight, an asset when wearing delicate or lacy fabrics.

When designing your jewelry, important factors to consider are strength and durability. The thinner the petals are, the more fragile they tend to be.

Ideas for Flower Pins

There are many sources for jewelry findings. Craft and jewelry-making shops offer jewelry supplies, and there are wonderful catalogs available that feature a selection of good quality jewelry findings.

Making Miniature Flowers With Polymer Clay

Project: Pansy Barrette

1 Make a Holder for Your Barrette

1. Crumple aluminum foil wider and longer than the barrette.
2. Press the barrette, with the top side up, onto the crumpled foil making a little nest to hold the barrette.

2 Prepare the Background

1. Knead and soften some green clay that is in the same color family as the leaves. Roll out, with a rolling pin or brayer, a strip of clay that is less than ¼″ (0.6cm) thick and a little wider and longer than the top of the barrette.
2. Press the center of the strip onto the top of the barrette to make a slight indentation in the underside of the clay. This will hold the clay in place on top of the barrette.

3 Arrange and Attach the Pansies to the Barrette

1. Embed the pansies and leaves into the clay strip using a small amount of tacky white glue.
2. After flowers and leaves have been added, look at the strip to see if it needs adjusting.

4 Bake Your Barrette

Place the barrette and holder into the oven and bake for twenty or thirty minutes at the temperature recommended for your clay.

5 Glue the Decorated Strip to the Barrette

1. When the clay is cool, remove the strip with the flowers from the barrette.
2. Glue it down with Goop glue.
3. Leave it in the holder until the Goop dries.

WHAT YOU'LL NEED

- Several prebaked pansies that are thick and strong
- Prebaked pansy leaves
- Unbaked green clay, in the same color family as the leaves
- Rolling pin or brayer
- A barrette
- Tacky white glue
- Toothpicks
- Goop glue

TIP

Baked pansies and leaves can be glued directly to the barrette with Goop glue without making the background strip. The background strip provides a more sturdy barrette.

Project: Daisy Pin and Earring Set

While the following instructions are for a daisy pin and earring set, the general method of making the jewelry is the same for any of the flowers.

WHAT YOU'LL NEED

- For the earrings: two prebaked, strong, similar daisies
- For the pin: one or more prebaked, strong daisies
- Prebaked daisy leaves
- Unbaked green clay, in the same color family as the leaves
- One pin back
- Two earring backs
- Tacky white glue
- Toothpicks
- Goop glue

1 Arrange Your Pin Design

Decide on the arrangement of the pin's daisies and leaves. Since each flower will be a little different, each design will be unique.

2 Prepare the Background Clay

1. Knead some of the unbaked green clay in your hand until it is very soft.
2. Roll the clay into a ball and place it in the middle front of the pin backing. Pressing from the center, spread the clay out with your fingers to the edge. Add more clay if needed.
3. Smooth the top of the clay and check to make sure that the green clay fits around the edges evenly.

3 Attach the Flowers and Leaves

1. Glue and press the daisies and leaves onto the clay in the pin back, embedding them into the clay. (Use a toothpick to put a small amount of tacky white glue on the middle back of each daisy and the lower part of each leaf bottom. Try to avoid seepage of the glue.)
2. If glue does seep out, wipe it away with your finger or a small piece of unbaked clay.

4 Bake Your Pin

1. Preheat the oven to the recommended temperature for the type of clay you are using.
2. Place the entire pin backing with the unbaked clay, the blossoms and the leaves attached onto a cookie sheet or stoneware plate.
3. Bake the pin for twenty to thirty minutes. Follow the baking times for the type of clay you are using.

5 Glue the Pin Back to the Design

After the pin has cooled, remove the baked clay from the pin back and glue it back into the pin with Goop glue.

1 Make Your Earrings

1. Glue the daisies onto the backings with the petals facing in a similar direction. Use Goop glue.

2. You will want to place the findings fairly close to the top of the daisy for better balance so they do not tip over when you are wearing them.

3. Most earrings are mirror images of each other. For these daisies it doesn't make any difference. If you were adding leaves, however, they would be positioned on each earring in a mirror image of the other.

ANOTHER METHOD FOR MAKING FLORAL PINS AND EARRINGS

1. Roll out, with a rolling pin or brayer, a flat piece of green clay or clay the color of the flower.

2. Cut a round or oval backing from the clay in the desired size of your pin.

3. Bake the clay backing according to instructions for the clay you are using.

4. Glue the blossoms and leaves onto the baked clay backing with Goop glue. Arrange the flowers and leaves so they overlap the edges of the clay backing.

5. A plain narrow pin back, such as the one pictured, can be glued onto the back with Goop glue.

6. For the earrings, a similar procedure can be followed.

7. Remember to place the findings close to the top so they don't tip over when you are wearing them.

More Ideas

I really like the choice of being able to use a treasured object, new or antique, elegant or primitive, to display the floral creations. In a formal setting, the flowers can add finesse to a decorative piece. Attached to country items, the flowers can be lovely or whimsical, and they add a touch of grace and beauty to weatherworn or crudely finished pieces.

Project: Wooden Boxes

The possibilities are endless when decorating boxes with flowers. Have fun creating your own arrangements. The beautiful wooden boxes shown here were handcrafted in black walnut, cherry and bird's-eye maple by my neighbor, Bruce Springfield.

This is an inexpensive papier-mâché box, with faux marbleizing sponged on and then sprayed with varnish. Roses, buds and leaves were attached to the box top with Handi-Tak.

Project: Container Arrangements

Besides the fun of creating the flowers and arranging them in pretty or unusual containers, foraging for small, unusual or pretty holders is a joy. Antique shops, craft stores, secondhand stores, garage sales and museums are all wonderful sources for unique and eye-catching containers.

Sources

The following retail stores are good sources for the products used in this book:

M.J. Designs, Michael's, Pearl, A.C. Moore, Ben Franklin, Total Crafts, Frank's Nursery and Crafts and Wal-Mart.

For beautiful boxes, picture frames and other objects hand crafted from fine wood:
Bruce Springfield
703-491-7840

Wholesale Companies:

AMACO
American Art Clay Co., Inc.
4717 West Sixteenth Street
Indianapolis, Indiana 46222-2598
(FIMO, Friendly Clay, Goop Glue, Friendly Cutters, Jewelry Findings)

Kemper Mfg. Inc.
P.O. Box 696
Chino, California 91710
(Kemper cutters)

Pacer Technology/Super Glue Corp.
Rancho Cucamonga, California 91730
(Handi-Tak)

Plaid Enterprises, Inc.
1649 International Court
Norcross, Georgia 30091-7600
(Plaid Tacky Glue, FolkArt Paint, Dry-Brush Stencil Paint, stencil brushes)

Polyform Products Company
1901 Estes Avenue
Elk Grove Village, Illinois 60007
(Promat, Sculpey III, Super Sculpey)

Shenandoah Framing
215 Greenhouse Road
Lexington, Virginia 24450
(Shadowbox and other frames)

Thomas Collectibles
P.O. Box 565
955 N. 400 W. Bldg. 6
North Salt Lake, UT 84054
(801) 298-8102
(Globes and Domes)

Wilton Enterprises, Inc.
Department F-1
2240 West 75th Street
Woodridge, Illinois 60517
(Cake decorating and candy making supplies)

Index

More Great Books for Creating Beautiful Crafts

How to Make Clay Characters—With polymer clay and imagination, you can bring cheery little clay characters to life. Brilliant, step-by-step projects progress in skill level—from simple Neighborhood Kids to a detailed Grandpa or Saint Nick. Expert clay artist Carlson, is well known for her "Wee Folk" polymer clay creations and line of collectible "Pippsywoggins" characters sold nationwide. *#30881/$22.99/128 pages/579 color illus./paperback.*

How to Make Enchanting Miniature Teddy Bears—With fuzzy fabric, a snippet of thread, and these clear instructions, you can start creating adorable little bears (only a few inches tall) right away! Ten projects progress from a simple teddy bear pin to a range of teddies with different styles and moveable limbs. *#30846/$22.99/128 pages/212 color illus./paperback*

Painting Roses with Deanne Fortnam—In this complete guide, decorative painters will learn to paint gorgeous roses the Deanne Fortnam way. In eleven step-by-step projects, this master decorative painter covers a wide range of styles, from simple strokework roses to Norwegian and Russian styles with detailed blossoms, buds and foliage. *#31107/$23.99/128 pages/309 color illus./paperback*

Creating Extraordinary Beads From Ordinary Materials—Transform the most ordinary, accessible materials into uncommonly beautiful beads! You'll be amazed at the fascinating array of beads you can create using these 53 step-by-step projects in a range of styles—and no experience or fancy equipment is needed! *#30905/$22.99/128 pages/326 color, 18 b&w illus./paperback*

Painting Flowers in Watercolor With Louise Jackson—Master decorative artist, Louise Jackson, shows you how to beautifully render one of decorative painting's most popular subjects—flowers! All you need is the desire to follow 15 detailed, step-by-step projects from start to finish! *#30913/$23.99/128 pages/165 color, 21 b&w illus./paperback*

Creative Finishes Series—Explore the world of creative finishing with leading decorative artist, Phil Myer! Each book features a variety of techniques, paint applications and surface treatments in 15 projects complete with detailed instructions, patterns and step-by-step photos.
  Painting & Decorating Tables—*#30910/$23.99/112 pages/177 color illus./paperback*
  Painting & Decorating Boxes—*#30911/$23.99/112 pages/145 color, 32 b&w illus./paperback*

Gretchen Cagle's Decorative Painting Keepsakes—Discover a treasury of beautiful projects collected from one of today's most celebrated decorative painters! In her latest book, Gretchen shares 31 of her all-time favorite projects. No matter what your skill level, clear instructions, traceable patterns and color mixing recipes will have you painting in no time! *#30975/$24.99/144 pages/91 color, 44 b&w illus./paperback*

The Crafter's Guide to Pricing Your Work—Price and sell more than 75 kinds of crafts with this must-have reference. You'll learn how to set prices to maximize income while maintaining a fair profit margin. Includes tips on record-keeping, consignment, taxes, reducing costs and managing your cash flow. *#70353/$16.99/160 pages/paperback*

Selling Your Dolls and Teddy Bears: A Complete Guide—Earn as you learn the business, public relations and legal aspects of doll and teddy bear sales. Some of the most successful artists in the business share the nitty-gritty details of pricing, photographing, tax planning, customer relations and more! *#70352/$18.99/160 pages/31 b&w illus./paperback*

Painting & Decorating Birdhouses—Turn unfinished birdhouses into something special—from a quaint Victorian roost to a Southwest pueblo, from a rustic log cabin to a lighthouse! These colorful and easy decorative painting projects are for the birds with 22 clever projects to create indoor decorative birdhouses, as well as functional ones to grace your garden. *#30882/$23.99/128 pages/194 color illus./paperback*

How to Start Making Money With Your Crafts—Launch a rewarding crafts business with this guide that starts with the basics—from creating marketable products to setting the right prices—and explores all the exciting possibilities. End-of-chapter quizzes, worksheets, ideas and lessons learned by successful crafters are included to increase your learning curve. *#70302/$18.99/176 pages/35 b&w illus./paperback.*

The Art of Painting Animals on Rocks—Discover how a dash of paint can turn humble stones into charming "pet rocks." This hands-on easy-to-follow book offers a menagerie of fun—and potentially profitable—stone animal projects. Eleven examples, complete with material lists, photos of the finished piece and patterns will help you create a forest of fawns, rabbits, foxes and other adorable critters. *#30606/$21.99/144 pages/250 color illus./paperback*

Painting Houses, Cottages and Towns on Rocks—Turn ordinary rocks into charming cottages, country churches and Victorian mansions! Accomplished artist Lin Wellford shares 11 fun, inexpensive, step-by-step projects that are sure to please. *#30823/$21.99/128 pages/398 color illus./paperback*

Painting More Animals on Rocks—Lin Wellford has introduced thousands of people to the unique magic of transforming ordinary rocks into imaginative words of art. The fun continues in this book as Lin shows you how to become your own "rock artist" by creating frogs, penguins, field mice, foals, bears, wolves and other colorful creatures. *#31108/$21.99/128 pages/290 color illus./paperback*

The Doll Sourcebook—Bring your dolls and supplies as close as the telephone with this unique sourcebook of retailers, artists, restorers, appraisers and more! Each listing contains extensive information—from addresses and phone numbers to business hours and product lines. *#70325/$22.99/352 pages/176 b&w illus./paperback*

Making Greeting Cards With Rubber Stamps—Discover hundreds of quick, creative, stamp-happy ways to make extra-special cards—no experience, fancy equipment or expensive materials required! You'll find 30 easy-to-follow projects for holidays, birthdays, thank you's and more! *#30821/$21.99/128 pages/231 color illus./paperback*

The Art of Jewelry Design—Discover a colorful showcase of the world's best contemporary jewelers. This beautiful volume illustrates the skilled creative work of 21 production jewelers, featuring a wide variety of styles, materials and techniques. *#30826/$29.99/144 pages/300 color illus.*

Making Books by Hand—Discover 12 beautiful projects for making handmade albums, scrapbooks, journals and more. Only everyday items like cardboard, wrapping paper and ribbon are needed to make these exquisite books for family and friends. *#30942/$24.99/108 pages/250 color illus.*

Make It With Paper Series—Discover loads of bright ideas and easy-to-do projects for making colorful paper creations. Includes paper to cut and fold, templates and step-by-step instructions for designing your own creations. Plus, each paperback book has over 200 color illustrations to lead you along the way.
  Paper Boxes—*#30935/$19.99/114 pages*
  Paper Pop-Ups—*#30936/$19.99/96 pages*

Make Jewelry Series—With basic materials and a little creativity you can make great-looking jewelry! Each 96-page paperback book contains 15 imaginative projects using materials from clay to fabric to paper—and over 200 color illustrations to make jewelry creation a snap!
  Make Bracelets—*#30939/$15.99*
  Make Earrings—*#30940/$15.99*
  Make Necklaces—*#30941/$15.99*

Acrylic Decorative Painting Techniques—Discover stroke-by-stroke instruction that takes you through the basics and beyond! More than 50 fun and easy painting techniques are illustrated in simple demonstrations that offer at least two variations on each method. Plus, a thorough discussion on tools, materials, color, preparation and backgrounds. *#30884/$24.99/128 pages/550 color illus.*

The Decorative Stamping Sourcebook—Embellish walls, furniture, fabric and accessories—with stamped designs! You'll find 180 original, traceable motifs in a range of themes and illustrated instructions for making your own stamps to enhance any decorating style. *#30898/$24.99/128 pages/200 color illus.*

The Best of Silk Painting—Discover inspiration in sophisticated silk with this gallery of free-flowing creativity. Over 100 full-color photos capture the glorious colors, unusual textures and unique designs of 77 talented artists. *#30840/$29.99/128 pages/136 color illus.*

Master Strokes—Master the techniques of decorative painting with this comprehensive guide! Learn to use decorative paint finishes on everything from small objects and furniture to walls and floors, including dozens of step-by-step demonstrations and numerous techniques. #30937/ $22.99/160 pages/400 color illus./paperback

Decorative Painting Sourcebook—Priscilla Hauser, Phillip Myer and Jackie Shaw lend their expertise to this one-of-a-kind guide straight from the pages of *Decorative Artist's Workbook!* You'll find step-by-step, illustrated instructions on every technique—from basic brushstrokes to faux finishes, painting glassware, wood, clothing and much more! #30883/$24.99/128 pages/ 200 color illus./paperback

Fabric Sculpture: The Step-by-Step Guide & Showcase—Discover how to transform fabrics into 3-dimensional images. Seven professional fabric sculptors demonstrate projects that illustrate their unique approaches and methods for creating images from fabric. The techniques—covered in easy, step-by-step illustration and instruction—include quilting, thread work, applique and soft sculpture. #30687/$29.99/160 pages/ 300+ color illus.

Paper Craft—Dozens of step-by-step paper craft projects to make, including greeting cards, boxes and desk sets, jewelry and pleated paper blinds. If you have ever worked with or wanted to work with paper you'll enjoy these attractive, fun-to-make projects. #30530/$16.99/144 pages/200 color illus./ paperback

Jewelry & Accessories: Beautiful Designs to Make and Wear—Discover how to make unique jewelry out of papier maché, wood, leather, cloth and metals. You'll learn how to create: a hand-painted wooden brooch, a silk-painted hair slide, a paper and copper necklace and much more! Fully-illustrated with step-by-step instructions. #30680/$17.99/128 pages/150 color illus./paperback

Elegant Ribboncraft—Over 40 ideas for exquisite ribbon-craft—hand-tied bows, floral garlands, ribbon embroidery and more. Various techniques are employed—including folding, pleating, plaiting, weaving, embroidery, patchwork, quilting, applique and decoupage. All projects are complete with step-by-step instructions and photographs. #30697/$16.99/128 pages/130+ color illus./paperback

Nature Craft—Dozens of step-by-step nature craft projects to create, including dried flower garlands, baskets, corn dollies, potpourri and more. Bring the outdoors inside with these wonderful projects crafted with readily available natural materials. #30531/$16.99/144 pages/ 200 color illus./paperback

Create Your Own Greeting Cards and Gift Wrap With Priscilla Hauser—You'll see sponge prints, eraser prints, cellophane scrunching, marbleizing, paper making and dozens of other techniques you can use to make unique greetings for all your loved ones. #30621/$24.99/ 128 pages/230 color illus.

Creative Paint Finishes for Furniture—Revive your furniture with fresh color and design! Inexpensive, easy and fun painting techniques are at your fingertips, along with step-by-step directions and a photo gallery of imaginative applications for faux finishing, staining, stenciling, mosaic, découpage and many other techniques. #30748/$27.99/144 pages/236 color, 7 b&w illus.

Everything You Ever Wanted to Know About Fabric Painting—Discover how to create beautiful fabrics! You'll learn how to set up workspace, choose materials, plus the ins and outs of tie-dye, screen printing, woodgraining, marbling, cyanotype and more! #30625/$21.99/ 128 pages/4-color throughout/paperback

Creative Paint Finishes for the Home—A complete, full-color, step-by-step guide to decorating floors, walls and furniture—including how to use the tools, master the techniques and develop ideas. #30426/$27.99/144 pages/212 color illus.

Creative Silk Painting—Uncover the secrets of silk painting as you get the inside story on how to apply brilliant color to silk and create beautiful art more quickly and easily. You'll explore exciting new topics, including new instant set dyes, creative painting techniques, creating garments and textile art and much more! #30713/$26.99/ 144 pages/120 color illus.

Stencil Source Book 2—Add color and excitement to fabrics, furniture, walls and more with over 200 original motifs that can be used again and again! Idea-packed chapters will help you create dramatic color schemes and themes to enhance your home in hundreds of ways. #30730/$22.99/144 pages/300 illus.

Paint Craft—Discover great ideas for enhancing your home, wardrobe and personal items. You'll see how to master the basics of mixing and planning colors, how to print with screen and linoleum to create your own stationery, how to enhance old glassware and pottery pieces with unique patterns

and motifs and much more! #30678/$16.95/144 pages/200 color illus./paperback

Decorative Painting With Gretchen Cagle—Discover decorative painting at its finest as you browse through pages of charming motifs. You'll brighten walls, give life to old furniture, create unique accent pieces and special gifts using step-by-step instructions, traceable drawings, detailed color mixes and more! #30803/$24.99/144 pages/64 color, 36 b&w illus./paperback

Painting Murals—Learn through eight step-by-step projects how to choose a subject for a mural, select colors that will create the desired effects and transfer the design to the final surface. #30081/$29.99/168 pages/125 color illus.

Painting Baby Animals With Peggy Harris—Now you can paint adorable baby animals with the help of professional oil painter Peggy Harris! You'll learn her fun, exciting and virtually foolproof method of painting using 11 color, step-by-step projects that show you how to paint a variety of realistic little critters—from puppies and kittens to ducklings and fawns. #30824/$21.99/128 pages/319 color illus./paperback

Handmade Jewelry: Simple Steps to Creating Wearable Art—Create unique and wearable pieces of art—and have fun doing it! 42 step-by-step jewelry-making projects are at your fingertips—from necklaces and earrings, to pins and barrettes. Plus, no experience, no fancy equipment and no expensive materials are required! #30820/$21.99/128 pages/126 color, 30 b&w illus./paperback

Holiday Fun Year-Round With Dian Thomas—Discover how to turn mere holiday observances into opportunities to exercise imagination and turn the festivity all the way up. You'll find suggestions for a memorable New Year's celebration, silly April Fool's Day pranks, recipes and ideas for a Labor Day family get-together, creative Christmas giving and much more! #70300/$19.99/144 pages/150 color illus./paperback

Other fine North Light Books are available from your local bookstore, art supply store, or direct from the publisher. Write to the address below for a FREE catalog of all North Light Books. To order books directly from the publisher, include $3.50 postage and handling for one book, $1.50 for each additional book. Ohio residents add 6% sales tax. Allow 30 days for delivery.

North Light Books
1507 Dana Avenue
Cincinnati, Ohio 45207

VISA/MasterCard orders call TOLL-FREE
1-800-289-0963

Prices subject to change without notice.   Stock may be limited on some books.

Write to this address for information on *The Artist's Magazine*, North Light Books, North Light Book Club, Graphic Design Book Club, North Light Art School, and Betterway Books. To receive information on art or design competitions, send a SASE to Dept. BOI, Attn: Competition Coordinator, at the above address.

8548